KNOW YOUR WORTH GODDESS

THE EVERYDAY GODDESS REVOLUTION

KNOW YOUR WORTH GODDESS

ISBN: 9798528749020

THE EVERYDAY GODDESS REVOLUTION

Dedicated to awakening one million women around the world to their potential.

www.theeverydaygoddessrevolution.com

KNOW YOUR WORTH GODDESS

CONTENTS

KNOW YOUR WORTH GODDESS

FREE RESOURCES

Join our FREE Goddess Academy and access over $2000 worth of free training and resources.

https://everydaygoddessrevolution.thinkific.com/courses/GODDESS

HALEY

It can feel like being swamped in an ocean at times can't it, this journey of worthiness? There are times in our lives when we are gently bobbing along the surface gliding with the waves, the warm sun dancing on our skin. Yet, during others, we find ourselves pulled by the current and plunged into the murky depths, unable to see clearly with nothing but the sound of water rushing in our ears. And, just like the flow of the current or the turning of the tide, it can change one way or the other, in a moment.

Achievements and relationships can bring us validation and boost our self-esteem, while betrayal or abandonment are devastating and leave us feeling that there must be something intrinsically wrong with us. This ocean is unpredictable, and no one ever knows which way the tide will turn.

It has taken me a long time to figure this out. So many years spent battling the elements, only for me to realise that in the same way that healing is not linear, as cyclical Beings we tend to spiral along with nature. And just as the tides ebb and flow in conjunction with the waxing and waning of the moon, so does our human experience. If someone had told me this at the start it would have saved me a lot of heartache, and money. For I was always searching for "It" – the one thing/workshop/book/teacher/modality etc., that would teach me the magic formula on how I could wholeheartedly love myself. How I could root myself in my own light and worthiness.

I exhausted so much of my energy, painstakingly looking outside of myself, giving my power away, without realising that the simple fact of my very existence itself declared my worthiness and fully whole-ness. A fact that was constantly being mirrored back at me from every corner of the universe. I will say that one more time for the people in the back: *the simple fact of your very existence itself declares your worthiness and fully whole-ness.*

We cannot separate worthiness from who we are, for it is woven into the very fabric of our Being. But it is easy for us to be blinded to it. Dysfunctional families, disempowered parents, abandonment, toxic relationships, and abuse, amongst other trauma, all plant the seeds for unworthiness. Respite from that constant low-level, nagging feeling that we are just not enough is sought in addictions, eating disorders, shopping, mindless scrolling through social media, and binge-watching TV. Anything to numb the discomfort, anything not to have to feel.

This is when we know that the current has swept us under. We are engulfed by feelings too big and uncomfortable to process and yet the more we engage in those behaviours, the more it increases those feelings of unworthiness. Enter guilt and shame, and with all three firmly in cahoots, we find ourselves stuck on the hamster wheel of self-loathing in a perpetuating cycle of low self-worth.

As dark and despairing as this may seem, hope can be found through the process of awakening. And I do not mean awakening in the somehow-always-just-out-of-reach enlightenment sense but through the subtle opening of our awareness. This enables us to tune into the many reminders that surround us all day, every day. You see, self-worth is straightforward and once understood makes intuitive sense but has somehow become over-complicated and therefore difficult to grasp.

We have been conditioned to believe that we need to seek external experiences in order to gain insight into who we truly are, or to validate our sense of worth. But the simple truth is that real magic is found in our everyday ordinary experiences. The warmth of a sleepy child, the smell of coffee and cake shared over conversation with a good friend, the beauty of the setting sun, the smile of a stranger, the unfurling of a fern towards the light, the countless number of stars freckled across the night sky. These are all examples of ways in which our worthiness is being reflected back at us.

The things we deem sacred are mirrors of our own inherent sacredness. The beauty and majesty that we witness in myriad ways during any normal day is the same beauty and majesty we carry in every cell of our bodies. But nobody took us to one side and told us that. There was no self-worth class at school. As a result, many of us have struggled for most of our lives trying to figure it all out.

Of course, the big question is *how* do we get ourselves to this point of understanding? I propose that we must dare to believe it and give ourselves permission for it to be true. While diving deep to excavate the patience and tenacity required to come back to it time and time again. Until we have fully awakened to the realisation that *we* choose the value that we place on our self-worth; no one else has that authority or power.

Any time we need reminding, we can listen to the breath, which is constantly affirming our existence and right to take up space. Or we can choose to focus on any number of ways in which the wonder of nature represents our splendour and individuality including, at the most fundamental level, how we move within our own internal cycles and seasons.

The rhythmic rolling of the waves reflects our ability to adapt and change.

The rumble of thunder symbolises our innate power, strength, and courage.

The magnificence of the sunrise mirrors our unique gifts, talents, and sense of purpose.

The dance of the wind represents the spirit that moves us. The same spirit that asserts with every breath cycle just how valid, needed, and oh-so-very worthy we are.

This journey is not linear. We will ebb and flow, rise and fall. Our tide will be high one moment and low the next. That is why we must learn to ride the wave of resilience whilst deeply anchoring ourselves in acceptance. That is why our self-worth can never be dependent on anyone, or anything, but us.

Haley Blackman - From reiki master to crystal healer, yoga teacher to priestess of Avalon, workshop facilitator to women's circle creatrix, practitioner of tantra, embodiment coach, amateur women's spirituality historian, closet artist, mother, and lover of the simple things; I've played many different roles over the years, but my 'thing' is teaching women who long to be wild how to live a more authentic and liberated life through the healing arts of yoga, tantra, and embodiment.

www.wildwomanology.com

BUCKSO

Still, even today, the thoughts will try and permeate the barrier in my brain. NO! Stop right there! You know you are not allowed here, don't you? Haven't we gone through this already? For goodness' sake, it is 48 years down the line, and I am still having these conversations with myself!

It does not go away for good ya know. That voice, that little knot that forms in your gut at the mere thought of stepping into the POWER of who I am. It starts with doubting whether I am able to 'pull it off', this new idea I have about my life and business. It is further compounded by those around me. When I DARE to share my thoughts with them, and I feel myself slipping into the falsehood of their beliefs. Then I start reasoning with myself as to why it is "probably best I let it go". That is when we need to shout out…STOP!

Do not allow those thoughts to spiral into something tantamount to you convincing yourself that the murder you just read about, is somehow your fault! It is laughable really when you think about it, isn't it? What we tell ourselves? And dependant on the timespan of these conversations, can lead to us taking FULL responsibility for all of life's eff ups, eh?

Anyway, I digress. The point being, given long enough, these lies we tell ourselves day in day out will eventually convince you that you ain't worth ANY type of success or fulfilment in life at all, whatsoever.

That is because over many years, as kids, we had NO choice but to sit and listen to conversations pertaining to 'lack of' and 'making do'. Or that we 'should be grateful'. Constantly hearing elders talk about ALL the tough times; or the hardships such and such is going through; and just how TOUGH life is, leads us to forget we ever even had a chance to think any other way.

When we turn into adults, we continue to perpetuate these beliefs. We shut ourselves off from any other way of living life. Then, we carry on doing it out of guilt for our parents/family cos, 'Well they worked SO hard for us all to eat and have a roof over our heads'.

WRONG!!!

They also did not realise there was another possibility for them. Because they TOO carried on living life the way THEY were brought up to believe was the only way. And so on and so forth…

We ALL have a God-given birth right to live a life of TRUE abundance and prosperity and yes, YOU ARE WORTHY! You are fully entitled to DO what you like, LIVE how you like and BE just how you like. YOU get to make ALL the choices you want for YOUR life. The thing is we are never told this by anyone. It is only as we get older and choose our friends more wisely that our minds broaden and open up to new possibilities.

I grew up in exactly this kind of environment and there is just ONE thing I must say here. This is NOT a chapter of blame. I am FULLY aware and respectful of ALL the things my parents went through, as first-generation immigrants to the UK. They had VALID reasons to be who they were. It was a game of survival for them.

But the thing is, my life started to become that in MY mind, and there really was not ANY need for it to be! But you feel this GUILT for even daring to think any different, all out of some misplaced loyalty.

ALL it is, is that you KNOW better! You just KNOW there is more to life than what is presenting.

That was EXACTLY my thing. I saw a new paradigm for me. But all along the way, while I was forging this new life for myself, I had the self-talk going on, on repeat. Telling me that I did not deserve an easier life after what I DID!

After I left home, I made decisions that my parents were not happy about. From my mid-20s I spent a LOT of years constantly berating myself for the way I had done things. As mentioned earlier, the length of time and the severity of how we talk to ourselves WILL have an impact on our self-worth. WE get very good at doing it to ourselves, to save anyone else doing the job, of course!

It took a LOT of inner work to finally convince myself that yes, I AM WORTHY of having this life of less stress, less grief, and less turmoil. I GET to choose that. Another person's truth is NOT mine. I know this now. And however sad I feel for that life story and narrative, it is NOT mine to continue carrying forward. I DO NOT deserve to carry that burden.

It is imperative that YOU know this too. In your life, you may be feeling all of these emotions, but there is no need to take them on as yours. Be really discerning and recognise just who's voice is playing out when you tell yourself things that you KNOW, deep down, are not true. Find those folks you can be totally honest and open with. Oftentimes, they are not your family! And that is OK.

The journey I am inviting you to take is one where I encourage you to live a life where; you never make another person wrong; to always speak and live, in YOUR truth.

If you are not sure what that might be, get the help.

Ask for help and find a mentor or coach that will show you the way to fully explore your worth. In time, the conversations you will be having with yourself will always end with you knowing, I AM WORTHY!

Buckso - Buckso is a Spiritual Coach/Practitioner & Actor. Through her life she has acquired a myriad of skills that serves those individuals who have dreams, ambitions, and desires of their own, whatever line of work they're in. Those looking for direction and support that may be missing for them for various reasons such as an unsupportive network, friends, family and social circles or a lack of direction. Spirituality has played a big part in Buckso's life and she's been on her own quest for the last 30 years, knowing there was more to this existence than met the eye.

www.bucksodw.com

DEANNA

Why it is time to overcome self-doubt and release those limited beliefs so that you can follow your joy and create the life of your dreams.

So many of us are on a journey in life to discover who we are.

There is a quote by Denis Waitley that resonates with me.

'It's not who you are that holds you back, it's who you think you are not.'

This is very true. Those feelings of unworthiness hold us back and stop us from going after the dreams and aspirations that can help us feel truly happy; to live a life of joy and abundance.

My journey has been incredible, but it has not been without its struggles. For most of my life, I have battled with my weight. At various times, it has caused low self-esteem, lack of confidence, and no sense of self-worth.

In my early 20's I worked in call centres and sales. Although I was good at these jobs, I did not enjoy them. I wanted to do the things that made my heart sing; the things that brought me joy. I knew that I wanted to help people. I was drawn to all these spiritual and woo-woo things, and I loved doing card readings. Deep down, I knew that this was not accepted by the people around me. I was expected to have a 'normal' job. Getting up and going to work. So that is exactly what I did.

I became so unhappy that I suffered from severe depression. I lost my jobs due to my mental health. I was so unhappy with my life, I had days where I did not even want to get out of bed. My health began to deteriorate because I was not looking after myself properly. It was the wake-up call that I needed. I realized that I needed to value my health and who I am. We only get one shot at this life, and we have to make the most of it.

I started looking into how natural and alternative therapies could help me. I found my way onto a course to train in Reflexology. I loved it; it was the starting point for me to train in a range of healing and alternative therapies.

I would not be here now, doing what I love and working hard to qualify as an acupuncturist, had I not gone through that awful time in my life. As I reflect upon it, I realize that at the time, it felt like I was having a breakdown. Nothing felt like it was working. But the truth is, it was a breakthrough. Sometimes, when you are in a dark place, you think you have been buried, but you have really been planted.

You are Worthy

Your self-esteem and self-worth are connected. Self-esteem is how you see yourself, and self-worth is how you value yourself; it is that deep understanding that you matter.

Even the most successful people harbour doubts about themselves. As a therapist, I meet many people who feel like impostors. They are not, and sadly it holds them back.

Why do we worry so much about what other people think? When we worry about what other people think of us, we give our power away; we dim our light.

Ask yourself, what would you do differently if you did not care about what other people think?

In our society, it is common for people to be conditioned to care more about what others think than what we think of ourselves.

The truth is you *are* worthy of love, happiness, abundance, joy, and anything else you wish to have.

There is a beautiful quote by Rumi that says,

"What you are seeking is seeking you."

That is so true; we just have to align ourselves with what we want to have, be, and achieve.

The Power of the Goddess

Never underestimate how valuable you are. You are important; your thoughts, feelings, visions, experiences, all matter.

You cannot be important to people all the time, but you can be important to yourself. You have everything you need within you to learn to love and accept yourself. You can be your biggest supporter.

Your self-worth is deeper than your self-confidence because it is knowing who you are on the inside. Embracing your truth, accepting yourself for who you are.

As you learn to know, accept and love yourself on all levels you can connect easily to your inner goddess.

Who are you deep down?

How would you describe your real self?

The power of love and kindness is enormous. Sharing it with others can help change the world and make it a brighter place. But we must also extend that love and kindness to ourselves.

Give yourself permission to feel good and enjoy the things in your life, focus on the things that lift you up.

You are capable of amazing things

Another quote that resonates with me comes from Thomas Edison;

"If we did the things we are capable of, we would astound ourselves."

There have been times in my life where I have not done the things I have wanted to do because I felt unworthy. When I look back now, not only could I kick myself, but I wish that I had not wasted those opportunities.

Instead of shying away from new challenges, I now try my best to embrace them and figure out how I can push myself; learn more about myself; grow and meet each challenge with as much success as possible.

Growth can be painful, but it can also liberate you from staying stuck. You will never know what you are capable of unless you believe in yourself and go for it. Sometimes, it may seem impossible, but there is always a way.

Take that step. You will never fully be ready. But you are capable of learning. You are capable of growing. And ultimately, you are capable of amazing things and worthy of more.

Deanna Thomas - Founder of Deanna Thomas Therapies. A multi-talented therapist specializing in Healing, Energy Work, Tarot, and Essential Oils. A certified Spiritual Medium & Angelic Reiki Master Teacher, Aromatherapist, Advanced Crystal Therapist, Reflexologist, and Wellness Advocate.

https://linktr.ee/deanna27

EMMA

I never felt worthy.

When I look back over my life and try to define a moment that I lost my sense of worth, there is none. I simply never felt worthy.

This is not a tragic storytelling; as a child, I was very loved by the people that surrounded me. I had a wonderful childhood filled with happy memories. I have so much gratitude for my upbringing in so many ways, but there is a very, *very*, distinct void when it comes to feeling worthy. Worthy of that love and that life. It took me a long time to recognise the reason for that void.

My dad never made me feel worthy.

I was unworthy.

Unwanted.

Unlovable.

My parents separated when I was only a few months old. I was the only little girl in my class who did not live with her daddy. A class full of daddy's girls.

My dad came from a long line of men that were not particularly paternal and had no idea how to show love *or* how to entertain a school-aged, chatterbox of a girl. The daddy's girl I craved to be, never got to exist.

Seeing so many other girls my age with amazing fathers who protected them and idolised them left me feeling less than. I wanted to be protected by the giant man that would never let anyone hurt me. Not having that protection left me feeling vulnerable. At risk. Unprotected.

Was I not as pretty and lovable as the other little girls?

Why didn't anyone want to protect me?

I joked one day, when my dad met my first proper boyfriend, that my dad would kill him if he hurt me.

My dad replied,

'No, I won't. That's your problem, not mine.'

Not protected.

Not lovable.

Not worthy.

For the first half of my 38 years, I tried in vain to get my father's attention and love.

Do not be too noisy.

Do not be too loud.

Do not be too…anything.

But even being less than was not good enough.

I did not try hard enough.

I did not strive far enough.

A lost cause. A missed opportunity.

A fickle, fair weather, silly girl.

For the next 15 years of my life, I stopped trying.

I settled into life.

I settled into marriage.

I settled into my job.

I settled into motherhood.

I settled.

I lived inside my mediocre, not too much, not enough box, and I was happy…for a time.

Until I wasn't.

Until all that too much,

Too loud,

Too big and bold and beautiful,

Started to bubble up inside me. It forced me to burst out of my mediocre box and confront my non-conventional, entirely too weird, and too much for social norms self. It shattered my marriage in the process and disappointed my dad…again.

18 months later I received the news that my father had cancer.

18 months after that he was home in the UK for the first time in several years and his diagnosis was terminal.

Between myself and my sister-in-law, we cared for him until the end.

For the first time in my life, we had time together to speak, and listen. And we did. Often. About all the good times and all the bad. All his mistakes and all his successes. His measurement of a life well lived and how his diagnosis had changed that for him.

He asked questions about me and listened to the answers.

I saw love in him for the first time properly and I saw fear.

Not just fear that he was dying.

Fear that he could not go back and do it differently.

I learned forgiveness in those months.

True forgiveness.

I became a daddy's girl. Not for myself, but for him. For the man that tried his best to raise me and failed more times than he succeeded. I put my pride aside and became the dutiful daughter. This time not doing it to prove to him that I was lovable, but to prove to him that *he* was loved.

I saw that the story I told myself about my own worth, as measured by my father's inability to be present, was just that, a story.

I was not unlovable.

I was the daughter of a man who did not know how to show me I was loved.

And *that* was very, very different.

I realised my worth the day I bent down to tie his shoelace as we left for a hospital visit. I do not remember a time when the roles were ever reversed but I suppose they must have been.

This man, so proud, so strong, so untouchable by the world, needed me to tie his shoelace. There was so much worth in that small act of kindness. There was so much love in a moment of huge vulnerability.

I did not need anything else.

My father taught me that I did not need anyone to make me feel worthy. He taught me to seek that worth within myself. And he taught me how worthy I was because I saw the frightened little boy inside the man.

By the time I said my final goodbye to him, so much had healed. His death was like a rebirth for me, and I know he stands behind me now reminding me I do not need anyone's affection to be lovable.

I do not need anyone's protection to be strong.

I do not need anyone's approval to be worthy.

I am worthy.

Emma Halley is a Crystal Therapist, Spiritual Wellness Coach, and Intuitive Healer with more than 20 years' experience. She teaches people all over the world how to find alignment and flow so that they can find their way back to the joy and love that is within themselves.

www.thecrystalmoonmentor.com

HILLARY

Understanding your own worth through relationship with self

We hear about self-love all the time. I mean...all the time. I am guilty of overusing the word in my coaching practice for sure. Not to mention my hashtag obsession with it on my social media, memes...shall I continue?!

Let's break it down.

Your worth is directly related to your relationship with self. Yes, your relationship with yourself. Your worth is 100% from within. How you treat YOU.

I know, right? I can almost hear you thinking 'uhhh, yeah no.'

I feel you. Truly, I do. There was a time in my life that I too believed that my self- worth came from those around me; those I loved; even the eyes of a stranger as I passed by. I believed my self-worth was generated from the outside in.

Living this way felt like an emotional, volatile, and blissfully moody way to exist. I measured my worth based on the mood of those around me whose opinion I valued most. This method of measuring myself was nothing short of absolutely awful. I mean, on the days when I received attention and praise from others, I felt elated. I had hung the moon. The world was my oyster and every other nauseating play on words imaginable. It was like being high.

But then, the attention would fade or turn elsewhere. The compliments would stop coming in, at least in the story I played out in my mind. Every time this happened, I would hit an all-time low. Each and every time. Leaving me scraping my worth from the floor below me. And just like that...

The attention returned, and with it my view of my own self-worth.

Are you starting to see a pattern? Is it ringing true for you? This pattern kept me from understanding my value. My own worth.

It was not until I saw the pattern in how I kept handing the power of my worth over to others that I became realized that I could not ride that emotional rollercoaster anymore. It made me too dizzy.

I started questioning myself. Why had I allowed others to decide my value or lack of it? I allowed them to define my worth. So, what was my worth anyway, I wondered. It was at this point in my life, when I was at the lowest of lows on the self-worth scale, that I had an epiphany. I had been a coach and in the wellness industry for over a decade, I knew this stuff!

The epiphany? I saw my relationship with self. Looking in the mirror, I no longer saw the mom, the entrepreneur, the adrenaline-adventure-seeker. I saw a sad, broken woman. Unhealthy, overweight, and without belief or hope. Unable to move on.

'Hope. Hope is BS. Hope comes from a lack mindset, Hillary.' I thought.

Yes, I had practiced and taught. Hell, I even embodied it at one point! I knew this! I could do this! The veil lifted and I saw self-doubt like a mile long garbage dump that I had ignored and allowed to fester into a whole field of BS.

Belief system? A rather limited belief system. I knew I needed to treat myself better. It was time to ask myself out and evaluate our compatibility.

The simplest way to evaluate your relationship with yourself is to ask yourself the following questions:

1. Would I say (*insert what you have just said to yourself, i.e. 'You are so fat', 'They will never love you that way'...etc.*) that to the love of my life? How about my child? Or my parents? My best friend? How about a complete and total stranger?

2. Would I do that or treat my love, child, parents, friends, or strangers by (insert; *missing Dr appointment, yoga class, not eating all day long, say you will do something and not, say you will be somewhere and not show up*) The list could be endless!

Remembering to ask yourself these simple questions is key to gauge our awareness of how we value ourselves. To understand our worth. To remember YOU ARE WORTHY

Now we need to look at the answers and change what needs changing!

What did I do to change things?

I dated myself. Treated myself how I had believed others should, or even how I wanted them to treat me. You know, back in the day when I allowed others to decide my worth. I knew I was worthy.

For me, it looked like me becoming my best friend. Holding my hand when I was frightened to step out into the garbage dump of trauma. She not only held my hand, that girlfriend jumped on the loader and started shovelling that shit out of there! She let me take breaks when I felt exhausted from the work and encouraged me when I wanted to quit. She raised her hand to shout 'Hell Yes!' to the things I/she had always dreamed of having. There was a lot of inner work, energy shifting, tears, hugs and yep, you guessed it...self-love...because I AM WORTHY.

That's right. Self-love is understanding that our relationship with ourselves is how we define our self-worth. Defining that YOU ARE WORTHY. Only we can name our worth. We teach others our value. Our worth is defined by how we view ourselves. It not only comes from within but is developed from the love we give ourselves in the relationship with self. This is self-worth. This is self-love. The understanding that the power to our worth is ours and ours alone.

Can you find your worth overnight? Sure! Why not, the power is Yours.

Can you do it without shedding a few tears? C'mon, I could fill a swimming pool with the tears it took to grow into a healthy relationship with myself! In understanding that I AM WORTHY. Will you too?

The fact is YOU ARE WORTHY. Every relationship looks different, doesn't it? No two are the same. We each have a unique life experience. Embracing that uniqueness is a key component of embracing the love we have for self. Think of it like this; the love of your life is like no other. You see their worth with such ease.

Others may resemble them, a sibling, a twin perhaps...and yet, that twin is *not* your life love, are they? No, your love is. In all their uniqueness you find them worthy. There may have been some rough patches here and there, but you are committed to communicating clearly and in a loving and honest manner, correct? So... be your life love. Experience your self-love as your own soulmate. Be your ONE TRUE LOVE and know YOU ARE WORTHY

Hillary Sepulveda Brown is committed to reminding 1 million women globally that they are the ONE TRUE LOVE they have been searching for! Hillary is a 45-year mom of 5, Nana of 1. An international wellness entrepreneur, nonprofit founder, and leader for over 20 years in the wellness community. Hillary is a lifetime yogi holding her E-RYT 500 with Yoga Alliance, world traveler, innovator, and motivational coach.
Often labeled as an idealist, Hillary believes in shining our light and being exquisite from the inside out.

www.hillarysepulveda.com

HOLLY

A few years ago, I had to leave my husband while I was pregnant, I was terrified and vulnerable. My pregnancy hormones meant I wanted nothing more than to feel safe and protected, I wanted to nest but had to leave my home. My husband subsequently left the country, accepting no responsibility for his son emotionally, practically, or financially.

This led to a lot of soul searching. Although it was obvious that my husband had made a lot of mistakes, I knew I would not gain anything from blaming him. I would not learn from this unless I took some responsibility.

Looking back, I could see it should have been obvious and predictable that he was not ready to be a father. Why had I hidden it from myself? How could I have chosen so badly? I had genuinely believed he would make an excellent husband and father; how did I get it so wrong?

It can be our darkest places that bring us to discover ourselves fully. Being alone and pregnant was a wake-up call for me.

Through therapy, I discovered a deep sense of not being 'good enough/worthy', which affected all my thoughts and behaviours. It made me too nice. I was nice because I did not feel I was worthy of my own opinion, or of saying no. I was terrified of conflict and never even acknowledged my own needs.

People described me as tolerant and accepting. I had never considered asserting boundaries for how other people treated me. I rarely felt angry. I had periods of deep sadness, but I tried desperately to get out of them as quickly as possible.

I had underlying anxiety about most social interaction, even with my closest friends and family. But I pushed those feelings down and smiled through them. People praised me for being so positive.

I felt it made them want me in their lives, my sense of identity was invested in being nice and positive, I could not be anything else. I was nice because I did not think I was worthy, that I would not be accepted and loved otherwise.

With a lot of introspection and support, I have discovered a secure and authentic me. One of the many steps in my transformation was when I started asking myself 'If I believe I am good enough, how do I think/feel/behave in this situation?' It was transformational. My perspective completely changed.

Now, I can ask for help when I need it. I have better, deeper friendships than ever before. I do not need a social mask; I do not need to be interesting; funny; nice; or positive. I can just be myself in that moment. I understand and express my feelings respectfully but assertively and put in clear boundaries that support and protect me. This does not create conflict but creates understanding, and an ability to care for one another more fully.

Contrary to what I previously assumed, the more I speak up, the more open and honest I am, the more people like me, the better connections I have, the better decisions I make, the more fulfilled, whole, and authentic life I can live.

Grounding yourself in a sense of worthiness is not a quick process, if you are also on this journey, I want to leave you with a technique that I use often that you might find useful.

This technique is based on Neuro-Linguistic Programming (NLP) Parts work. Here two different examples of how it might be used:

Example one - processing emotions:

Recently I was feeling very sad about a potential relationship that did not work out. I noticed I was trying to repress that feeling, trying to distract myself. I was telling myself not to be silly. So, I stopped. I sat down. I put my hand on my heart and I allowed myself to cry for as long as I needed. Then I asked that area of my heart, what it wanted for me.

Why did it want this love?

If I had that love, what would I have that was even better?

The answer was safety. I wanted to feel safe.

21

Then I asked myself in what other ways could I feel safe. I realised that I could do grounding meditations, manage my money better and do exercise that got me more rooted in my body. All these things give me a sense of safety and so that part of me that was feeling sad could be satisfied.

Example two - changing behaviour:

This is useful because when our behaviours are misaligned with our values it affects our self-worth.

I was going through an incredibly stressful time, and I started comfort eating cookies. At some point, I recognised that although it gave me a serotonin rush for a few brief seconds, it did not fit with the values I had established for my health. So, overall, it was making me feel worse.

I was able to identify that a solution for this was to join a gym. It aligned with my values, was a healthy option and made me feel good for much longer than a cookie did.

Try using this strategy on yourself for a behaviour you want to change.

This is simplified NLP Parts work - the full process (6 step reframe) is easily available online if you want to explore NLP more thoroughly.

1. Identify the unwanted behaviour (in this case eating cookies)

2. Establish the positive intention of the unwanted behaviour (in this case feeling happy, forgetting about all worries)

3. Think of at least 3 different ways you can get the positive intention in healthy ways (e.g., dance, watch a comedy, read a good book, go to the gym)

4. Choose one and do it instead

5. Enjoy

Holly Kobe Aye Ashi - I am a person-centered therapist, I have a variety of skills I utilise depending on the client's needs. These techniques include hypnotherapy, occupational therapy, neuro linguistic programming, yoga, and meditation.

KARISHMA

It is 8th May 2021, and I am sitting here writing this book, a book that is actually going to be published and sent out to the world to read. Am I worthy of writing a book? The old version of me would listen to my thoughts and say 'No!' But the new version of me believes that I will write this and trust that it is going to unfold beautifully with ease and grace, because I am worthy of being an author.

Who gets to decide whether you are worthy? People out there? Your parents? Your partner? Your friends? Your colleagues? It is down to you to recognize that you are worthy! It is not always easy because in some ways you do not even know that your worthiness needs addressing, just like me.

I was taken back to a moment in time, years ago. A moment that made me realise how much I undervalued myself as a teenager. All because of a group of people in school. I look back now and think 'How dare they determine my worth?'

Now I understand it was not down to them, it is what I allowed them to do. For 2 years I was continuously bullied in school in the UK. It was a complete shock to my system as I had grown up in Zambia in Africa where I had not encountered bullying.

When I was bullied, I held it together in front of them. But deep down inside I was allowing them to damage me. I got through every day by calling them 'lower than fungus'. Do not ask why as I have no idea where I even got that from!

The more I thought about it, the more I realised that I had suppressed so much emotion and what they instilled in me was this sense of smallness, unworthiness, a sense of lack. I had carried this with me until one day I decided to release the trauma and I was taken to a vision of me taking my power back, I decided that I get to make the choice of how long they get to keep me down.

I choose now! Now is the time I stand my ground for my rightful place on this planet. I am someone who will not be taken down by external circumstances. I get to choose the life I want to create, and it is not one of victimhood.

My sense of worthiness has always been affected by what I considered to be my default – a victim mindset. For the longest time I could not see any way to live other than as a victim. Living with the thought that no one ever wanted to hear what I had to say. I felt that I was unlovable; that everyone around me was in a relationship when I was not; that success was for other people. Where I was in life just was not good enough. Depression seemed justified because I was not worthy enough to be happy. I even questioned my worthiness to be a coach. Who am I to teach and coach others and help them transform their lives? How ridiculous!

The truth is we are infinite beings. We all have every potential to achieve greatness.

What is it that you want to achieve?
Do you feel that you are worthy of it?
Your dreams, your desires?

Again, I ask, who gets to determine that you are worthy? It is not as simple as your boss, friends, family, or anyone else showing you. It is about you getting to a place where you can face your past and uncover what caused you to feel unworthy in the first place. You were not born unworthy. Get that straight first and foremost.

Let us crack open the true essence of what makes you worthy.
Is it the house you live in, or is the home within you?
Is it the watch you wear, or the time you share serving the highest good?
Is it the little you have, or the size of the impact you make in the world?

It is essentially you who gets to make that choice. There is no one out there who is so much more powerful than you, that they get to stand on you and weaken you.

Lessons come through the people we meet and the circumstances that show up in our reality. Oh, the universe does like to test us! It took me a while to connect with the fact that I am worthy. I would not be here sharing this precious moment with you otherwise.

Now I am confident. I get to say I am worthy of teaching and sharing with others.

The best advice I could ever share is to tell you to learn to accept yourself. Look into your eyes and see beyond that outer shell, see the beauty underneath your skin.

Start to reclaim the power that you gave away to your own version of bullies by releasing those trapped emotions that you might not even know are there.

My journey has taught me so much. I want to encourage you to realise that *you* are the creator of your reality. You determine how you show up for yourself. It is not down to someone else to determine your worthiness.

It all starts with you, from within you.

For the longest time, love was something that I stayed shut off from. It seemed too big. Something that was not for me. It was only when I received guidance, thanks to my higher self, that I realised that I had a fear of love. It was surprising but it explained a lot.

At that point, I felt the words 'You are worthy of love' just flowing through me. How divine! I just said to myself, you are so right! I am worthy! I just kept repeating it to myself and at that moment, I felt it ignite within me.

Even as I write this chapter, the energy of powerful love is flowing through me and everything I do. Feel it as I send the beautiful energy for you to feel because just like me, you too are worthy of love from yourself and others.

You are worthy of being loved, heard, seen, acknowledged, happy, empowered and so much more. This is the true essence of who you are. It is time to feel it, believe it, embody it, be it.

Sending you so much love, light, gratitude and well wishes.

Karishma Sharma - Karishma is a Spiritual Business Mindset Coach, Breakthrough expert, Energetics Queen and an International speaker. Karishma Sharma is in summary a life transformation advocate.

www.karishma-sharma.com

KATHRYN

I transformed my life, physically, emotionally, and mentally and significantly improved my self-worth through an understanding of brain science and the role my brain was playing in my tainted perception of myself.

I had a history of depression from a very young age, that lasted on and off into my 30's. The anxiety crept in during motherhood in my early 30's. Despite having a successful career in IT spanning 2 decades, a loving husband, 2 beautiful children (I now have 3) and a nice home, I still lived in a world of inner anguish. Anguish created by my own internal state.

Daily I failed to trust myself. Or trust my own opinions. My internal narrative was toxic. Despite having strong instincts, I would ignore them and seek answers outside of me. I had trouble making decisions for myself and would constantly ask other people what they thought. I would not just ask one person, I would ask multiple people. Then I would sit in a confusing mess of different opinions, completely unable to make a decision for myself.

I was forever thanking other people for 'everything they had done for me/the project/the team' and never stopped to acknowledge my own contributions. There was a part of me, a very connected, wise, and spiritual part of me, that I kept hidden for fear that people would think I was weird or had lost the plot. All of this stemmed from my incredibly low self-worth, an inability to trust myself and failing to love myself for who I was.

In my early 30's I had an incredibly powerful Aha moment at a seminar where I learned about the body's biological response to stress. I learned that we can get locked in our fight or flight mode, particularly if we have experienced trauma and especially if that was childhood trauma.

This knowledge explained some physical aspects I had been experiencing but could not yet make sense of. That single interaction unleashed a curiosity about neuroscience and a yearning to learn more about my own brain and the role it was playing in my life.

During my neuroscience training I learned some real nuggets of wisdom in relation to the biology of our brain:

Our thoughts travel along neural pathways in the brain and the thoughts and habits we have been repeating for a **LONG** time create really **STRONG** connections in the brain. Counter to that, new thoughts and new habits hold weaker connections which is why it is so easy to fall back into old habits - the old pathways in the brain are much deeper, stronger connections!

Our brain is what is called 'plastic'. This means we have the ability to change our brain structure, our thoughts and our habits by changing our wiring. Two of the ways I did this were through a pattern interrupt and mindful awareness.

Some of you reading this chapter may be able to relate when I say I had a toxic inner critic. It presented itself in many ways.

Stepping on the scales and berating myself for the number I saw

Punishing myself for starting a "diet" and then eating something "not allowed"

Sending a work email and constantly ruminating that I should have said "x" differently or not said "y" at all.

Freezing at the most important moment in meetings and being unable to speak, despite knowing exactly what was required at that moment.

Constantly replaying interactions from my day and whispering 'you are an idiot Kathryn, you don't know what you are doing, you are hopeless'.

Did you know that as humans we can turn on the stress response with our thoughts alone?

I learned this piece of wisdom from the amazing Dr Joe Dispenza. When we have thoughts like the ones above, playing on repeat all day long, it triggers our fight or flight response and that's just damn exhausting. Both physically and emotionally harmful.

Pattern Interrupt

With my new understanding of the brain and our wiring, I decided to use a pattern interrupt technique to change things up. When the old pattern of my inner critic would drop in, I would stop and notice the thought (mindful awareness) and then replace the harmful thought with a deep breath and simply say to myself "I love you, Kathryn".

In the beginning, I would have been saying this up to 30 - 40 times a day, maybe more. Truth bomb, I felt like a lunatic telling myself I loved myself multiple times a day, yet it is funny how I never thought twice about any of the toxic thoughts I used to circulate on repeat.

The act of doing this practice meant I was rewiring my brain for Self-Love!

Mindful Awareness

In the brain, we have two networks or modes of operating.

The **default network** is the one where our thoughts just wander all over the place.

The **direct network** is where our thoughts have focused attention.

When we are in the *default network* it is easy for the negative thoughts, that bring our sense of self-worth down, to seep in and take over. Being mindful of our thoughts allows us to catch when we are heading in a downward spiral and to use tools like pattern interrupts.

For me, using these techniques over time meant that the negative thoughts started to dissipate. We do not 'disconnect' old wiring in the brain fully, so those thoughts can still come back. But using a pattern interrupt technique allows us to stop going down the toxic inner critic super-highway and allows us to mindfully choose to create the ***new wiring***. This facilitates us to create positive habits, thoughts, and patterns in our lives. It literally allows us to change the story we are telling ourselves.

When we are holding on to the negative, and old thoughts, patterns, and habits, there is rarely any room for the new that we want to bring into our lives. Some of you will have a yearning, a deep inner knowing that there is more to life. More to your journey and purpose than what is being expressed today. But when we spend too much time with the thoughts that we are not worthy there is no space to create miracles in our life.

It is much harder for my inner critic to bind me or hold me back from living life as my true authentic self. To stop me from following my dreams. Moving the dial on my self-worth has enabled me to value my own opinion and trust my internal guidance system. To learn to celebrate me and my contributions to the world and to step into my power and value who I am.

Kathryn Van Der Steege has 10 years of Neuroleadership theory and application, and a Brain-Based Coaching qualification with over 200 hours of coaching experience. Kathryn has a deep passion for working with individuals to understand their own triggers and how they can bio-hack their brains and emotions to maximise their potential. Having experienced depression from before the age of 10 and through to her 30's where the anxiety kicked in and having transformed her life mentally, physically, and spiritually Kathryn has a deep desire to show others experiencing the same kind of anguish that there is another way.

www.kathvdsmindset.com.au/

LAURA

Every day you have a choice whether to listen to the voice in your head or not.

I know first-hand that the voice is often unpleasant. I have often identified myself as a perfectionist: someone who is scared of failing and who does not feel good enough in every area of her life. So where does this lead me? You got it!! I am unworthy.

Unworthy of so many things. Because I am just not good enough. My inner critic is quite the nag, reminding me thousands of times a day, consciously and even more subconsciously that I am unworthy. Unworthy of love; happiness; success; and good health. We all have a belief system that holds that inner critic who informs us and the universe every moment of every day.

The truth is we all feel unworthy at some point in our lives. These feelings are typically formed in our early years due to traumatic events. Once they are believed by the subconscious, they are stored like files in a databank. The databank holds all your beliefs, your memories, your skills, and your previous experiences. Everything that you have seen, thought, and done are also stored there.

Some of you may immediately recognise events that have been traumatic. Others will say, 'I have not had anything traumatic happen to me'. Most people hear the word 'trauma' and think of the big T's; abuse, tragic events, global disasters etc. But many of us do not realize that we all carry little T's with us unconsciously.

31

Up to the age of 7, our brains are unable to rationalize our experiences. For instance, when I was 6, I was playing with my neighbour one day. I wanted to stop playing and go inside and he did not want me to. He blocked me from getting up the stairs to my back door. I told him that if he did not let me pass I would bite him. He did not let me go, and yes, I bit him. I went inside but soon my mom found out what had happened.

I was told to go and apologize. When I refused, I was asked to sit on the back porch until I did. This may not have been exactly what happened, but that does not matter. Because in my mind it did, and it was a traumatic event for me.
In that moment I decided that I was unworthy of expressing my feelings, that I was not heard or understood, and I was not worthy of having my needs met.

This was only one event. Can you imagine all the limiting beliefs we create around events like this? What we decide about ourselves, others, and life?

'I'm not worthy', 'I'm not loveable', 'I am never going to be happy'.

All these beliefs are carried in our subconscious mind. They replay over and over, and manifest circumstances in our lives. The good news is, there are several ways you can conquer the inner critic.

Steps to conquer your inner critic:

Step 1

Identify the limiting belief, so you can get to the root cause. You can do this by:

- Doing your inner/trauma work
- Meditation
- Journaling
- Learn more about how your mind works.
- Programs like Cognitive Behavioural Therapy can help you find the limiting beliefs.

Step 2

Release the limiting belief. This can take some time depending on the technique used. Through trauma work, you can often identify and release the beliefs during the same session so I feel this is the most important work you could do. Other ways to release the beliefs are to:

- Write them down and either burn or tear them up.
- Spotting them and knowing in your heart they are not real.
- Re-writing them
- Inner (child) work
- And of course, trauma work.

Step 3

Reprogram your subconscious mind. This can be done in so many ways. Many refer to this as a daily spiritual practice and can include:

- Visualization.
- Meditation combined with Affirmations.
- Mental movie.
- Gratitude.
- Journaling.
- Learning to understand how your mind works.

I know you may be thinking that all this is easier said than done. I totally understand that. I still struggle with my inner critic on a daily basis. Even when things all seem to be aligned, she sneaks in there, quietly whispering to me. But I have also observed the power in this work and know it is totally possible to shift and minimize the negative chatter.

I do believe that there will always be an inner critic. It is vital, in a way, to keep us safe, help us reflect and review circumstances that inform us of which decisions to make.

Mastering the mind, being aware of your thoughts and their patterns will become more natural the more consistent you are. Then you will have the super mind-screening power to filter through your thoughts and get rid of the ones that do not serve and keep the ones that do.

Remember every day that you can choose to listen to the voice in your head or not. Just observe your thoughts, without judgement. Remind yourself that the negative, critical ones are not true. Immediately positively re-frame the thought and state it as the truth.

KNOW YOUR WORTH GODDESS

You are worthy.!
You are loveable!
You are worth doing this work.

By doing all this work you will reach self-actualization, which is the complete realization of your true potential. You will transform, heal, and fully develop your innate abilities and appreciation for life.

I invite you to embrace your worthiness, identify and release those limiting beliefs, choose to reprogram your subconscious and tell that inner critic to take a hike!

Laura Dempsey - I am a Self-Actualization Practitioner and Reiki Master. I spent 20 years working in social services supporting, educating, and advocating for singles, seniors and families. I worked primarily with those who experienced mental illness and addiction by providing crisis support and suicide intervention. I have combined that knowledge and experience with the teachings of universal law, science of mind and spiritual principles. Now, in my coaching practice, I guide people who feel they can't get ahead, by showing them their true power within; by healing trauma, and by reprogramming their subconscious mind to live the life of their dreams.

www.true-transformative-healing.com

LISA

The Power Is Within You

Self-worth is my birth right but growing up I forgot this. I did not value myself.

Or my unique way of doing things, my own voice. The beauty and the power of me, exactly as I was. I gave my power away.

I was a girl that was lost in pain, anguish, and heartache, after abuse and trauma. Always looking outside of myself for validation that I was liked, loved, and worth it. That I was good enough.

Because my self-worth, self-love, self-belief, and confidence were zero.

In later life I looked for the validation I craved in my relationships and friendships. Always trying to get others to complete me, so that I could believe I was valued and visible.

But did it lead to me jumping for joy, to me being truly happy?

Heck no! Motherhood happened, and with it came the stress of looking after four young children, three with additional needs, with no support. And a husband who was a serial cheat, a family & friends who thought because I was smiling, I was ok, but the curveballs kept coming.

But here is the thing I have realised.

Curveballs happen. But it does not mean you have to let them define you
But for a very long time, I did

I had to reach the point where I realised that it did not matter what I
achieved. It did not matter how many certifications I gained. It did not
matter how many goals I set and reached. It did not matter how hard I ran
on the hamster wheel of life.

Nothing on the outside was going to fill the emotional hole in me.

All the loss, the hurt and the anger I had stored inside of me was working
against my energy flow. Because I refused to let go.

It was exhausting trying to prove to everyone else that I was worthy.

It took getting mind and heartsick for me to finally look at myself and say
enough is enough! There is more to my life, more to me, than this.

You may ask, why I am being so hard on myself. Truth is, I am just being
honest. With you, and with myself.

I had to spend time with myself, look inside me. To find my self-worth,
self-compassion, and discover my voice. To learn my own value.

The change did not happen immediately. I was still stuck in the middle of
all the curveballs being thrown at me. Accepting the good and the bad. Still
feeling like an outsider. But I had begun to see things differently.

Because nothing and no one on the outside could give this to me.

I decided: No more people-pleasing. No more trying to be someone and
something I am not. No more telling myself that I am not enough.

It was time to accept and embrace ALL of who I am.

I needed to put boundaries in place, raise my standards. Change how I let
myself be treated. Treat myself better. I needed to stop giving my power
away.

I was the person who was always nice, kind, loyal and loving. A giver in
every sense of the word. The girl who did not argue back. Who kept her

mouth shut. Who never used her voice. A mother, wife and friend who was always there.

Did all this bring me joy, love, a sense of worth and completion? NO! Because in lots of ways I still felt intimidated. Not enough.

I had forgotten about me. I had forgotten to treat myself with the same level of love, & respect, that I had, and still do give to others. I finally got tired of feeling this way, of feeling less than, of feeling not worthy.

I decided to start taking my power back, to reclaim me. Start being the woman, I have always wanted to be.

It is working. I am being more compassionate with myself. Recognising my own needs. Leaning into working with my own energy levels, and how I feel each day.

Now I ask myself.

'How does this feel? Does it make me feel good?'

'Does it bring me joy, love, happiness, does it light up my soul?'

If the answer is not 100% yes, it does not happen.

Before I would have carried on regardless, but now I am stepping into all that I am. My words, energy, heart, and soul are my superpower. And that empowers me to show up in a way I never would have before.

Because now I know I am worthy. I am enough, exactly as I am. I always was.
I get to choose my story; choose how I talk about myself; choose how others treat me. I get to choose my own reality.

I no longer need anyone else's permission to be me or to show up and shine in my life and business.

I know now that it was always up to me to believe in me. I always had the choice to change my thoughts, habits, and beliefs, that the woman I was, and am, has everything in me already, to be limitless.

Now, this is not to say the mind monkeys do not still come out to play, that would be a lie. They do, but I know it is because they are trying to keep me in my comfort zone.

But without ever taking risks, without new growth, I will never discover my infinite possibilities.

Journaling and meditation have been two ways I have been able to quieten my mind monkeys, reach my buried soul visions, and have the courage to write about everything I really wanted. To be the woman I truly want to be.

My worthiness, my enoughness, was always there, my power was already, and always had been, inside of me, all along.

If I can leave you with one thing:

You are you! You do not need permission from anyone, to do you! To live your life, your way.

You are enough, WORTHY is your birth right.

Lisa Martin - Lisa is a Soul alchemist, heart-led empath, writer, creator, who empowers introverted heart-led midlife women to reclaim their identities, to like, love & trust themselves, to gain confidence & self-belief, to rewrite their stories, and craft a life & business they truly want, by their own design, and their own soul rules.

www.instagram.com/the.lisamartin

LORETTA

I was daddy's little princess. Then my parents divorced when I was still very young. I was very sensitive and totally aware of the tension in our home. Before I could understand what was happening, my dad was absent, choosing instead to move in with another woman and her four children. His 'new family.' I felt abandoned and internalized all my feelings and emotions. I no longer felt worthy of love.

I carried those feelings of distrust and abandonment into my marriage and my former relationship. Inside I was numb, outside it looked like all was well. I felt like a failure and not deserving of love. Not knowing how to communicate my feelings, I kept silent, afraid of getting into an argument. Those relationships were very unhealthy and eventually ended.

But something positive came out of my marriage. I was blessed with three amazing sons. They kept me going, along with 'knowing' the universe has my back. All I ever wanted was to be a mother and my children are my world. They gave me unconditional love and the inspiration to live a better life, for myself and for them too.

My Spiritual journey towards healing and self-love took place after my divorce and the unexpected passing of my oldest son. I was traumatized with grief and sadness. As bad as things were, those significant losses set me on a path towards healing. Everything lined up serendipitously.

I was divinely guided. I dove deep into my core wounds, seeking freedom from the emotional pain I had endured. I had met many healers along my path. I became a Holy Fire Reiki Master, a certified spiritual guide and participated in a mediumship circle of women for nearly 10 years. As they

KNOW YOUR WORTH GODDESS

say 'healer, heal thyself,' and that is what I did. I was guided back to myself, my spirit soared, and I became free.

It became evident that forgiveness was key for me to move forward. Forgiveness does not mean that you approve of someone's actions, it means that you decide that you will no longer carry around those toxic emotions. Do those toxic feelings and emotions still arise? Absolutely, but I have the tools to recognize them when they do. I acknowledge them. That is the power. They do not control me anymore. I had to heal that inner child, that little girl inside of me who had experienced so much grief, trauma and pain but was bursting at the seams to be seen.

She had a voice that needed to be heard; needed to feel safe and secure once again. I have learned self-acceptance and self-love, and I have deep gratitude for my life just the way it is.

As the 13th-century Sufi mystic poet RUMI once said,

'The wound is the place where the light enters you.'

My journey brought me full circle when I lost my home. I had nowhere to go. I would never have dreamed that it would be my dad who came through for me. He offered to share his home with me for as long as I needed a place to stay.

At first, it was very difficult to express my feelings to him. But as time went on, I found the courage to share how I felt when he left me and my two brothers. I told him how sad I was when he did not come to visit. He explained that because mom was so protective of us, he did not feel comfortable enough to visit.

Dad was very open and receptive to my feelings. He also was open to sharing his feedback with me. From those conversations, we realized how alike we are. It is not uncommon for us to read each other's mind and complete each other's sentences. The open communication that my dad and I have shared, and the opportunity to express my true feelings have been a gift that I will always treasure.

We have laughed and cried, and our relationship has reached new heights. Some of the things he says to me now melt my heart. Love transcends all. Once his little princess, I now feel like a Divine Goddess woman who is worthy of love and embraces her power. I set healthy boundaries and I have a voice that speaks my truth. As I surrender to life and its magic and wonder, miracles and abundance show up everywhere. It is amazing how when you clear all those limiting beliefs about yourself, your innate gifts, intuition and talents just rise to the surface.

As I embrace the Divine Goddess within, my wisdom about life and all its experiences have brought me back to wholeness. I am my authentic self. I have turned my pain into purpose. My service is to create a safe space to rebirth soul-based change thru Conscious Grief and healing the holy womb chakra as a Holy Fire Reiki Master practitioner. Life is sacred. Enjoy every moment for it is a gift. As I connect and commune with my heart, soul, womb and the spiritual realm, my light shines bright. For I am never alone on this journey of expansion.

I Am Worthy, I AM.

Loretta Cristando Holton - As a modern-day mystic, I use my innate gifts and wisdom to connect and help support you on your souls' journey of remembrance. My service is to create a safe space to rebirth soul-based change thru the Akashic Records, Mediumship, Conscious Grief and healing the holy womb chakra as a Holy Fire Reiki Master practitioner. Holy Fire Reiki is a spiritual energy that creates wholeness, healing, empowerment and guidance. Author of -The Journey of Expansion -A Mother's Journey from Loss to Eternal Love

Www.openyourhearttospirit.com

LOUISE

Find your Voice, Speak your Truth.

At the age of 13, a girl started to take the mickey out of how quiet I was when I spoke. It seemed quite harmless, but from that day on I promised that I would never speak up because no one would hear me.

Little did I know that a choice I made 35 years later would be a lightbulb moment that changed my perspective forever.

I am not a massive fan of talent shows, but I sometimes find myself scrolling through the best auditions to give myself the feel-good factor.

I discovered a 19-year-old girl with a back story about being bullied for her singing. Her name is Jillian Jensen. Turns out she is a big fan of one of the judges, Demi Lovato, who was also bullied. She has the same tattoo. 'Stay Strong'.

As she sings, you can see the pain she feels from the experience of being bullied. She cannot quite believe that she is still here. You can tell that standing on that audition stage is a pivotal point for her. From now on she will be able to say, 'Stuff you, look at me now!'

The judges all cry. Simon Cowell tries to keep it together by eating crisps. Demi goes to comfort Jillian as she breaks down. You can see what it means to her as well. (I'm not crying, you're crying).

No one is going to get this girl down again. She stepped on that stage and is truly shining her light. Until that moment, she had no idea it was even possible.

Suddenly I am remembering all the incidents from years ago that have stopped me from shining my light. They play like a movie in my mind. Friends falling out with me; making fun of me; not sitting with me on the bus. Not knowing when it would stop. Giving away my power and feeling lonely. Making a promise to myself not to speak up.

At that moment I realise that each one of those seemingly insignificant incidents had, on some level, made me step back from allowing myself to be seen. Stopped me from taking the spotlight; shining my light and saying, 'look at me!'.

Not just then but until today. I had based my self-worth on what other people thought about me.

On top of all of that, I was always the posh girl from the village. But I lived with an alcoholic father, and a mum with bipolar, who was regularly submitted into psychiatric care. My life looked nothing like the rosy life that everyone thought I had.

I never received praise for what I did. Never felt loved at home. I bottled up my emotions. Even when I did well at something, I never felt good enough. This later manifested as a need to always try harder, until I was exhausted and at the point of burnout. At work, at life and in love. I desperately wanted to succeed in all of them.

I would reach a point in my career where I was doing well, and it would all start going wrong. The same with relationships. I put it down to there being something wrong with me, to not being good enough. I did not deserve to have those things.

Somewhere along the line, I loved myself enough to find my soulmate who became my husband.

After 25 years, I left my corporate job and set up my own well-being business. A spiritual awakening connected me with my Native American ancestors and powerful healing within my DNA. I understood my true purpose to enable those in the highest level of management to master their energy and emotions so that they could find joy and contentment; fulfil their true potential and get excited about the future.

My healing journey began with a release of emotions. I saw that growing up without an emotional role model meant I had never learnt to feel or express emotions like other people. There were a lot of tears and there still are. In the beginning, I saw this as a breakdown. Now I know that this is all healthy, positive, and releasing.

A bolt of lightning hit me on the day I watched that video. Despite all the inner and spiritual work that I had done; despite all the shadow work, the cleansing, the healing, and the transformation, when spirit whispered to me, 'You are powerful' I only thought, 'but they think I am not"

What a release! A promise to myself that nothing is going to dim my light again. It came with an intense divine feeling that I should fill my heart with love. Fill the space that had been taken up by fear of ridicule, shame, and embarrassment with love for myself. To know that the only person who needed to believe I had self-worth was me.

It was in a healing session, as part of my self-care, that I was guided to see the true expansion possible when you see yourself for everything that you are.

To see from the stars, the galaxy, and the universe. To see expansion, to see the mountains, the oceans, the forests, and the vastness of mother earth. To see the endless possibilities and unlimited opportunities that are open to you. To know that you are unlimited; that you are part of something bigger and that you are worthy.

Many people have become disconnected from who they are and their purpose. Conditioned by family, society, upbringing, events, and circumstances. When you start to play amongst the stars, then you realise that once you take your place, anything is possible.

You are used to being limited. For not taking credit for what you are doing. Only beating yourselves up or putting pressure on yourselves to get things right.

My self-worth had been dented by being bullied at school and feeling unloved at home. I also know that it goes deeper. Into many past lives where I have been persecuted as a healer.

I see people connecting to their self-worth by connecting to themselves as a human. One of my clients wanted to change their personal circumstances and we were talking through the process of her sharing it with her family.

As she was thinking it over, I just said, 'this decision is for you' and I felt the need to keep repeating it. When I looked at her, I could tell that she felt it and she believed it and she was worth it. That is why I do what I do.

Whatever has stopped you shining your light, give yourself permission to let it go NOW. You will not be stopped from taking the stage and being exactly who you are.

Sometimes life lessons come to us in the most surprising way. But there is always a reason, and it is usually the right time.

What are you waiting for? Go find your spotlight.

Louise Hallam worked in a corporate world for 25 years. After experiencing a spiritual awakening, she was connected with her Native American guides, who unlocked her true purpose and powerful healing tools. She now supports senior leaders and executives to eliminate stress and fatigue, by mastering their energy and emotions, so they can be more confident, their true self and rediscover the joy in their life and leadership. She holds the definition of success without struggle and connects humans to humans and to themselves. She is a channel for ancient wisdom and a spiritual mentor sharing this unique journey with women on a global scale.

www.stillcalm.co.uk

MIRIAM

Your body is worthy of your soul.

See me as I am

I look in the mirror
I do not look like myself anymore
Within
I feel so much younger

In the mirror I do not see a girl
But a woman
I look down on my body
It doesn't look
like I feel

- I have not been kind to you,
I say
I have not given you any credit
Was never satisfied with you
It is not your fault,
You respond.
It just happened

But we both know this,

it is not true,
It happened when someone decided
they had the right to my body

I ran away then.
And I dared not to come back to you

Then the transformation
Pulled me back into my shape
Where I am currently
on a voyage of discovery

- I Should love you more, I say
- I should take care of you
But then you answer me

See me as I am

And we both know this now
We are not in pieces
You are me.

I will reply

Here I was
Exploring
This magnificent creation
That was my home

No longer ignoring
No longer punishing
No longer escaping

I was opening my eyes
Seeing me as I am

Thank you,
I said to my body

Thank you,
it echoed back

I quite enjoy your company,
I said

I quite enjoy your company,
It echoed back

Here I was,
speaking to my body
Only to discover
It was replaying back
The exact same words I spoke

When I spoke of love
It spoke of love

When I was questioning its shape
It was questioning its shape

Why have I never seen this before?
I asked

48

Only to get the reply;

Why have I never seen this before?

I made the choice
Of choosing
The words
I wanted to hear

I am worthy

It was sneaking around
This feeling
of worthiness

It was never lost,
you see

I had only forgotten
it existed

There it was
Knocking on my consciousness

So I let it in

New words
started flowing
In my body
In my spirit

Together
we sang
the words
of worthiness

"I am worthy,
of loving my body

I am worthy,
of loving my soul

I am worthy,
of standing in my power

I am worthy,
of all my worthiness"

As the words pealed away
The layers I had built
It got clear to me
I am

created
of the same energy
That created
worthiness

The music of the soul

I read
a text
of people dying
with the music
within

Living life
where their song
was never played

Feeling
this was once me

I turned the music on
And dance for all those lives
A dance for all that music
That never was revealed
And never sung

As I danced
life started flowing
in my blood
in my body

An energy
so electrifying
it could have woke
those who never sang
And awakening
the music
of those
who are still here
In silence

Will you dance with me?
Will you play your music?

Will you let your self

enjoy this movement
of pure divinity?

Stepping into your body
with gratefulness
for all that it can express

The power of creative expression
will thank you
for being
fully you

Worthy
of singing
the song
of your soul.

Your body is worthy of your soul

Once I decided
I am worthy

I thought I was all good

That I would spend
the rest of my life

Knowing I am worthy
Knowing my body is worthy
Knowing my soul is worthy

I had to add another word
Compassion

You see,
sometimes I forget
my worthiness

There are days
where amnesia
pays a visit

These days
These moments
I have to remind myself

I am worthy, even when I do not feel it

Even on the days
You feel like
going back to bed
Screaming
Crying
Feeling angry

You are still worthy

A worthy body
A worthy soul
A worthy you

Is not measured in how it looks
what state of emotions you are in

Your body is always worthy of your soul
And your soul is always worthy of your body

And so it is!

As I step out of this poem
This chapter
In this book
Full of words of worthiness

I thank you for reading
I thank you for this moment together

To remember

To know the truth

Of worthiness

Miriam Stener is a spiritual coach and Auramediator coaching women to find their spiritual strength, heal their traumas, find their dharma and live according to their truth, passion, purpose and calling. Miriam is currently studying to be a Spiritual practitioner and later Dr. of Divinity within New Thought and Soulciété. Miriam is educated to university standard with her education in political science, language, communication, finances, and conflict management. She started her career in the online stock market at a Bank in Stockholm. Becoming a mother in 2009 she felt there was a missing part in her life, and she began her spiritual journey. Having to heal herself from sexual abuse as a child, she is now passionate about guiding other women on their healing journey. Miriam's spiritual interest combined with her corporate skills give her the experience to run workshops in four element profile in Norway and Sweden, as well as coaching highly committed people world-wide. Miriam's mission is to help 1 000 000 women create their own heaven on earth, overcoming traumas in this life and past lives. She believes that when we heal, miracles happen, and we can see our true goddess powers!

https://linktr.ee/miriamstener

NICOLA

A Wisp on the Wind

"The discovery that peace, happiness and love are ever present within our own Being, and completely available at every moment of experience, under all conditions, is the most important discovery that anyone can make."

- *Rupert Spira*

It took me decades to learn that worthiness is what I am and not something I need to find or something I can lose. For most of my life, I just did not match up to my own expectations.

You will be worthy when you are thinner; when your spots have gone, when you have a boyfriend. My teenage mind would remind me of this repeatedly. I cringe when I see my teenage self comparing herself to the models in the Littlewoods catalogue!

Later, my mind hooked onto qualifications, career, and motherhood. It hung on to the 'be thinner' chant too. It was an endless treadmill, my mind promising worthiness and happiness at some point in the future, if and when I met these unwritten expectations.

My mind innocently took on beliefs, patterns and expectations based on society, family, education systems and the time I grew up in. I was taught to do, get, and achieve, to be worthy. I was also taught which actions and behaviours would lead to unworthiness. What emerged from all of this was a cycle of pride, when I felt I was on target, and guilt and shame when I was not.

The curse of comparison was born. Not only was I comparing myself to others, but I also compared myself to my past self and the made-up expectations of my mind. It was a tangled web and there was a low lying and sometimes 'right in my face' sense of anxiety alongside feelings of unworthiness and dissatisfaction. Often, I did not feel safe, present or creative. Instead, I took on a tendency to hide. I believed that my escape route was to prove my worth.

The background mantra of my mind was 'Do I measure up?' Usually, the answer was no, and another search would begin to discover how I could change that.

Looking back, I can see that throughout my life, in times of joy and tragedy, I kept getting glimpses of a deeper truth about my true nature. Something much deeper and more profound than the content of my mind and the outward form of my life. In the glimpses, there was a knowing of the magnificence of each of us. The blinkers fell off and what was revealed was pure unconditional love in which the dance of life plays. Worthiness and unworthiness were seen to be an activity of the mind rather than an inherent quality of our being. Underneath the concept of worthiness, peace, happiness, and wholeness shone brightly.

Over the years, at times, this has been seen and experienced vividly. At other times it has been totally forgotten and that's okay – that is the perfection of waking up to the truth and then a veiling of that truth. Now I am much more fascinated by that within us that never changes, than the ebbing and flowing of the human experience. I can and do enjoy the humanness, but I know where home is, and I know what home feels like.

Home is unconditioned by any expectations of life and the mind. Its nature is wholeness, completeness, and unconditional love. Nothing needs to be added and nothing can be taken away.

Let me tell you a story…

A young woman had been lost deep in a dark forest for many years. For a long time, she had tried to find home, but in the darkness, it began to feel like a hopeless search. Over time she forgot about home and made the most of the forest. At times she was peaceful and content, but she often felt fear and a longing for happiness. She had a sense that there was more to life than this, but she had forgotten the peace of home.

Occasionally she would attempt to discover new parts of the forest but every time she did, terrifying gremlins would emerge from the undergrowth. The gremlins were disgusting, they stank, and they whispered dreadful things to her from the shadows. Time and time again she would retreat to the heart of the dark forest.

Until one day, while asleep on the leaves of the forest floor, she had an epiphany, an insight. She woke with a start, in her dream she had seen that no matter how many gremlins appeared or what dreadful things they said to her, not one of them had ever touched her. She sat quietly and dropped into the peaceful place within and then she stood and began her journey home.

Of course, the gremlins were outraged, the whispers became screams, they were relentless. As the days went on the gremlins became bigger and even more vivid, but undeterred the young woman followed her intuition and gradually made her way towards the forest edge. As she progressed, she noticed the gremlins beginning to shrink.

One day the screaming stopped, and they began to plead with her "please don't leave us". The woman hesitated, but just for a moment. With each step she took towards the light at the edge of the forest the gremlins became weaker and more transparent. As she stepped out of the forest into a beautiful clearing the gremlins became a mere wisp on the wind.

The young woman stood in the healing warmth of the sun and the peace of home flooded back.

The end.

Whatever form your dark forest and gremlins take I wish you all the love in the world as you uncover and remember home. My wish is for you to wake up to the inherent worthiness of who you really are and to abide in the peace and happiness of your being.

Much love,

Nicola

Nicola Drew is a qualified Psychotherapist and coach helping clients gain clarity and freedom of mind to overcome unhelpful symptoms, habits and behaviours. She also works as a trauma specialist helping clients overcome PTSD. Nicola has a special interest in the deeper nature of the human potential. She believes that every person has innate wellbeing which can be innocently veiled due to misunderstandings about who we really are and how life works.

Www.hippocoaching.co.uk

NICOLLE

Not if...Not When... But Now

'Worthy now. Not if. Not when. We are worthy of love and belonging now.
Right this minute. As is' - Brené Brown

I have spent my entire life not feeling worthy. Not worthy of love. Not worthy of close relationships. Not worthy of money. Not worthy of being seen or heard. And the list goes on.

One of the things I have learned over the years of being a trauma coach is that the one thing all humans feel at some point in their life is that they are not worthy of being who they truly desire to be. This is the common thread that links us all together and unfolds in every aspect of our life. The part that makes me so fascinated and determined to speak on this is that most of the world will die feeling that they are not worthy.

When I was a little girl, I always felt like I did not belong. I felt like I was born into the world with this heaviness of shame and unworthiness. But the truth is that it is my birth right to feel worthy of it all! When as a child do we lose this sense of worth?

When I was 16 years old my father took his own life. This set the tone for most of my adult life. I grew up with a lifestyle of abundance and wealth and seemingly had everything that I desired. Horses, a private school, a big house and so on. But I also never fit into that mould. I was the fat kid, the

60

one that hung out with the 'wrong crowd.' I was told that I would never amount to anything and pushed to the side quite often. I felt unseen and unheard.

I remember at a very young age that I did not want to live this way. I did not want money or success. I did not want to live in abundance. I will never be loved. People abandon me. It is not safe to be me. I am not worthy.

When we are young and traumatic incidents happen to us, we make a decision in that moment about ourselves, about life and people. Those thoughts become our beliefs and those beliefs create our reality.

So, with those beliefs stored in my subconscious mind, I lived a life of unworthiness. In all areas.

Throughout my whole life, I chose relationships that were toxic. I remember waking up the day after my wedding and thinking 'oh crap, what did I just do'?

I felt so unworthy that I naturally attracted someone who matched that energy and ended up marrying a man who was an addict. We were together for 10 years and spent those years completely broke and struggling, which is what I assumed I would become as a child.

I never finished school because I was not worthy of success, so it did not matter if I had an education. Everything I did carried a level of shame around the choices that I had made, and I felt like a total failure. I was an embarrassment.

I was constantly seeking validation outside of myself because I had no connection to who I was and what my potential was. When I moved through the world it felt heavy, like trudging through mud. I was broken. Spiritually, emotionally, and financially. And that was my truth. I was prepared to settle with that for the rest of my life.

And I am grateful for all of it.

I clearly remember the day that I was done with the suffering I had created in my life. Sitting at home one day I felt a shock go through my body that said there is something more and if I do not move and take inspired action I will continue to stay in my own creation and my own suffering.

The day it all changed was the day I asked for a divorce. It was a moment of power and knowing my worth.

I became obsessed with seeking truth in my life. It became my mission in life to take my power back and identify where I was handing my power over and where I was feeling unworthy.

I set out on my journey to awakening and on that journey, I found my purpose, my truth and my worth.

Through doing my own trauma work I learned how to use Universal Law to manifest and create what I truly desired. I began to shift my identity and embody the woman and coach that I was becoming. My beliefs began to shift, and I took full responsibility for the life that I created.

The Universal Law of Cause-and-Effect states that for every effect there is a cause. Meaning that everything I see in my life; all the suffering, all the lies, all the pain and all of the good were a direct cause of my own belief system. I created ALL of it. Heaven and hell on earth.

Once I chose to accept this law and know that it was fundamental to all of life, everything changed. I became the cause and recognized that I can create whatever I want. I get to remove the limiting beliefs that are swarming around in my head and keeping me stuck. I get to claim my power and step into my worth.

The truth is that you are worthy! And I am worthy too!

Love and gratitude
Nicolle Star xo

Nicolle Star - My mission is to Awaken the Sleeping Women. I help women to birth their purpose and calling, live on spiritual principle and live their truth.

https://www.nicollestar.com/

RACHEL

When I started to think about what I wanted to write for my chapter in this book, I began scanning the library of my mind for a defining moment that marked my embodiment of 'worthiness'.

I wanted that great big AHA moment. That moment in the movies where the music peaks. But even after much soul searching, the musical crescendo never arrived!

So, I asked myself;
'What does 'worthy' mean'?
Worthy of love? Being loved exactly as we are?
Worthy of belonging?
Having a loving supportive community of like-minded beings around us?
Worthy of receiving?
Getting richly rewarded for our efforts?
Worthy of living a magical life filled with the things we desire?

Or is it something else?

Is it the innate worthiness to BE - to identify as a child of the Universe? A being of love and light and complexity, on this crazy journey of life. A being that will sometimes get it wrong, but also sometimes gets it right.

What does 'worthy' mean to me? It is feeling like it is ok to just be me, in all my glorious imperfection.

You see, I am a recovering perfectionist. As such, 'worthy' gets wrapped up in a frosty blanket of being 'good enough'; of 'getting it right'.

Before I started my business, I am not sure I had ever thought of what it means to be worthy. I do not even recall hearing the term. It certainly feels like it has only become a thing in the last few years, anyway, as I squirrelled deeper and deeper into the burrow of modern Western Spirituality.

I may not have known the term, but I certainly knew what it was like NOT to feel worthy. I implicitly understood 'worthy' by experiencing the opposite. If the embodiment of 'worthy' is the full-colour photograph, then I was living the upside-down black and white negative of 'unworthy'.

I did not feel like I had anything of value to offer the world. I felt I had to perfect and refine the fundamentals of who I was in order to receive the love that I craved. The acceptance. At the same time, I felt like I was somehow better than everyone else as if I was in on the cosmic secret that they weren't. Like I had life all figured out because I was a devotee of the Universe.

I was not anchored in my power, so I was adrift in a sea of insecurity. I was caught in the schizophrenic tug of war of an Ego tearing itself apart from the inside. 'I'm too much. I'm not enough'. Between these two polemic factions was a being struggling to just BE.

Worthiness is a tricky beast. Until it is our time to unequivocally embody the frequency of worthiness, do we even know it is possible? Is it a Universal definition or is it personal to each of us? What does worthiness mean to you?

I now teach Sacred Self-Love, which is another way of describing the unflinching state and frequency of knowing that you are a Divine being, a manifest embodiment of pure and potent consciousness. That you are without a flame flicker of a doubt worthy of it ALL. Worthy of the Universal Love, your own love, the love of others, the safety, security, and unique embodied expression that is yours and yours alone to BE in this lifetime. Worthy of time and space and energy that is dedicated to you and the things that light you up. Worthy of respect and kindness. Worthy of compassion and Self-compassion.

What is Worthy? It is to know that you matter. That your needs and your happiness MATTER. It is knowing that your thoughts, your perspective, your voice, all matter. It is knowing that you do not have to do anything to earn the right to BE. It is a basic human right, to be exactly as you are.

When we start to embody the frequency of worthiness, we feel safe to take risks, safe to create, safe to step outside of our comfort zone. When we feel worthy, what we create is not tied to who we are as a Being.

The frequency of 'Worthy' is about our connection and embodiment of our own Divinity. We are each unique expressions of the Great Divine Consciousness, the heart within the Great Heart that Unites us all. We feel separate, but we are the Divinity that Unites. We are the Universal flow of Love and Loving consciousness.

When we anchor in this knowing, we are truly set free and empowered to be and do exactly what we wish. We do not seek approval or acceptance through any external action because we are fully anchored by the power of who we really are - the Universe having a human experience. The Universe dancing her disco dance in a human meat suit.

We can choose to interact with that however we wish, but this basic truth will set you free to experience your own unquestionable worthiness. You are the Universe in a meat suit, you have nothing to prove to anyone. Learn to love yourself my friend and let your power wash through every facet of your life, self-saturating light where only darkness lay.

You are worthy my friend - you always were. The parts of you that are at war are tethered to the small self. These parts need and deserve your love more than any, these are the parts that are hurting. These are the parts that are labouring under the false belief that they have to BE OR DO OR WHATEVER to receive the love that they long for.

Dear worthy one, you get to be that agent of love. Surrender yourself to the bliss-consciousness that is within you and marvel at how the healing balm of worthiness soothes every part of your soul.

There was never an AHA moment. There were never choirs of angels rejoicing that 'Rachel's finally got it!"

There was just moment after moment of saying yes to myself; of practising believing in my own worthiness; of turning back to my own Divinity every time my human self faltered.
There were many times of courage.

65

There were many times of saying NO to what did not serve.

And there continues to be.
Worthiness is your birth right. It is a practice, and it is an ongoing love affair with the Sacred in your Soul.

Your presence, your true eternal presence, is all that is needed to make a difference in the world. When you are worthy; when you love yourself as the Universe; you allow your true Divine frequency to shine forth and that frequency will not only affect you but also everyone that you come into contact with.

Don't wait for that AHA moment, start practising today.

Rachel Smithbone, aka the High Priestess of Sacred Self-Love and Spiritual Badassery, has a unique gift for creating deeply transformational energetic experiences. Rachel combines her diverse and original skillset as a qualified yoga teacher, gong therapist, intuitive energetic channel and natural sheman with her years of real world practical experience working in the Chairman's office at Goldman Sachs. When she's not cavorting round her ancestral farm on the Exmoor National Park, or playing in the ancient woodland with her hubby and two feral children, you can find Rachel offering bespoke 1-2-1 transformational coaching packages, sacred sound ceremonies and her online membership Yoga And Sound For Your Soul™

www.rachelsmithbone.co.uk/

RITA

I Am Worthy, I AM. **YOU ARE WORTHY. Because you are.**

WORTH DEFINED

I have always loved words. Their meanings, their history, and the connotation they take on in certain settings. Some words, like **WORTHY**, carry a depth of feeling, and a wealth of meaning. Even more so when someone is seeking a sense of worthiness.

From those few sentences, you may get a glimpse of how my mind works. I like to explore the meaning of things, take deep dives into the background of ideas.

I am a researcher and a soul-felt-feeler. I have been on a long journey to learn to understand myself better. Some things I learned brought me joy, but there have been times when I felt numb or in pain. Now, I value my spirituality and have a deep love for, and devotion to my children, grandchildren, and others I hold dear.

There are other special people in my life that I did not understand before. Because I did not value *myself* in the way I now believe all life is of value, I did not give the best that I could. I know now that I gave the best that I could at that time.

My internal growth was key. Sometimes I was so focused on my own ego's needs that I was blinded by them. When folks get stuck in ego, it is because they are having difficulty feeling WORTHY on the inside.

SO, ARE YOU, AM I, WORTHY?

While I was exploring my thoughts about WORTH, I found myself speaking to others about it too.

One friend shared that her feeling of basic fulfilment and gratitude for being alive made her feel worthy. She commented, "Although if I was isolated, or in a prison cell, I probably wouldn't feel very worthy."

Another noted that as she has grown older, her thoughts of worth have changed and deepened. She implied that now she looks internally for worth rather than seeking it through outside validation.

Mother Teresa is known throughout the world for her extreme gifts of love, charity, and restoration of life and dignity. She served and saved many. And yet, she was heard praying, rocking back and forth while on her knees, repeating these four words over and over. 'I am not worthy.' How could that be?

I am NOT GOOD ENOUGH

Your worth matters. Your truth about your worth matters. Your thoughts about your worth can change the trajectory of your life. It did mine!

"Are you worthy?" When you ask that question, what thoughts arise?

This is what was happening for me:

I am not 'good' enough because:

'You should not put yourself out there like that'.

'You are: too pushy; not smart enough; pretty enough; thin enough; powerful enough; connected enough; you are nobody special'.

'You should be thinking about others'.

Thoughts and feelings about my worth swirled. Some consciously, some not. Some accepted as absolute truth, but on examination, merely resulted from my particular conditioning, upbringing, or cultural norms.

With so many thoughts, patterns, and accepted messages at play for me, what was my journey to be?

68

A pivotal part of my life triggered a reassessment of self and my WORTH. This part of my story was not the beginning or the end of my journey but was certainly a game-changer.

I had never questioned the love of my children nor my husband. Family values were the foundation and framework of how my life was supposed to be.

I found myself loving someone so much. But I did not feel seen or cared for in a genuine way. It no longer felt authentic. Something was very 'off'. I was suffering and I felt lost.

After nearly 40 years of marriage, which at the beginning held friendship, love, laughter, and truth (as in soulmates), but it ended with pain. I was almost 100 pounds heavier, and literally, everything felt heavier.

DIVORCE.

There were missteps and mistakes on both our parts throughout our marriage. I believed that with mutual willingness and commitment to resolve our issues there could have been healing, restoration, and growth. But when I realized there had been massive betrayals over a long period of time, I had no choice. To live in my own worth, truth, and authenticity I had to step away and move forward.

This is not a story of victim or perfection, but of a journey many must take to understand and grow into our WORTH, empowerment, and purpose.

Spiraling into deep uncertainty and pain can serve to wake us up. It can suppress our soul's inner wisdom or empower it.

I decided to say yes. To more interests, more friends. My children were older and on their own life paths. It was time to forge ahead in WORTH and PURPOSE.

WORTH IS THE LENS FROM WHICH WE VIEW ALL ELSE

Your thoughts, your belief about your own worth in the world matters. WORTH is at your inner core affecting all outcome.

I believe for myself and others these are basic truths:

We are worthy because we are.

We are all worthy because we exist.

WORTH is our human collective starting point.

It is in our acceptance that **ALL** divine living creatures have true worth, that we most easily and comfortably embrace our own worth without judgement or qualifying conditions.

Our self-worth then determines the lens through which we see and judge the worth of others.

WORTH is a prerequisite for true voice, good relationship to self and others, healthy boundaries, and impacts the choices for all our possibilities. (I learned this the hard way).

MAKING PEACE WITH PAST is the only way to live in authenticity and compassion.

I have reached out for support and have been fortunate to have wonderful mentors, a good therapist, and beautiful caring friends.

I have learned I cannot plan exactly what may happen in my life. I can, however, determine how I want to show up. I feel worthy and empowered to do just that. I have learned to choose trust over betrayal.

I have made peace with my past, but challenging triggers still arise, sometimes unexpectedly. Now I have peace, worth, and strategies to move through them.

I am treasuring spending time with those I love.

I am sharing what I have learned with others who may benefit, working in partnership with a majestic, sensitive, 1200-pound horse!

During all the struggling and transitioning, it sometimes felt like I was sinking, but I remained determined and hopeful.

My first big 'solo' decision was to take a trip to Africa on my own, an enormous step for me. A dream trip to learn about elephants and their collective herd as we sat among them.

Later I adopted a Spanish Mustang rescued out of a kill pen in Colorado and named him the African word for hope: RAZA.

Rita Moore - As an educator I dedicated my long career to helping children, adults, and families receive the educational, social-emotional, and behavior supports they needed to thrive. I directed family support programs, served as an Exceptional Student Education Specialist, taught all ages and varying exceptionalities, provided district training, and taught Child Development and Testing courses at the college level.

www.RitaMooreCoaching.com

SADIE

Being a childfree woman, in a world that expects women to be mothers, can at times make you feel unworthy – as if somehow you have not fulfilled your purpose of 'woman' and have slipped into the realm of being other, one of life's edge dwellers with no certain place in society.

Every happy ending we see in every childhood fairy-tale; rom com; and popular TV show, typically includes a marriage quickly followed by a baby. The happy family is complete, and the woman fulfils her destiny. Reaching the pinnacle of female achievement - becoming a mother.

It is only in tragedies that the woman discovers she cannot have children – and it is portrayed as the worse fate to befall a woman. As for those who choose not to have children? We are the bitter spinsters; the evil stepmothers; the wicked enchantress who will tempt small children into the dark woods where she can gobble them up.

The narrative we are accustomed to by popular culture would lead us to believe that if a woman's worth is directly related to her ability to have children, then women who do not have children – through choice or otherwise – are therefore less than. Our worth is in question, our motives eyed with suspicion and our achievements always held up in comparison to the ideal of motherhood.

In a world that wants women to be mothers, being childfree is an act of rebellion. In my defiance of society's expectations, I am creating my own sense of intrinsic worth.

The expectations and rules of society are built on the patriarchal ideals of the feminine role being busy as the primary caregiver, so as to keep us diverted from seeking out power and fulfilment in our own right. Back to those fairy tales – it was those dangerous edge dwellers, living out amongst nature, the wild women, and the spell makers, who represented the biggest threat to the neat order of family life.

So, we were taught to be good girls. To do as we were told; not wander from the path (like poor Red Riding Hood); to fulfil the roles that were expected of us to receive the reward and recognition of societal validation. Complete the game in the right order and win the prize, right?

This was how I was feeling, and what I was struggling to find a solution for (so that I could live my childfree life without feeling a failure, or that I had to be constantly justifying my choices) when I discovered Lilith – the first woman – who taught me that I hold my own value, always.

Lilith was created at the same time as Adam, from the same mud and as such was created equal – something that displeased Adam greatly. His constant demands to be superior and for Lilith to be subordinate to him led to Lilith facing an ultimatum – conform to what was expected by her and stay in Paradise or choose to embrace her own wild nature and leave Eden to be free.

She chose to be free, and whilst Adam requested God make her come back, Lilith had stepped firmly into her own power and was having far too much fun being herself to want to come back to Eden and bend to Adam's will. So, being the ultimate patriarch, God cursed her – decreeing that all her children (also considered demons) would die – making Lilith the queen of hell and a mythical threat to children, babies, and pregnant women.

Lilith's story has many facets and lessons. What I have taken from it is that the idea of an independent woman, who values her innate wild nature, freedom, and equality, over the promise of a comfortable life conforming to the needs of others, is a terrifying thing indeed.

And I kind of like that because it takes back all the power of the idea of worth coming from an external source and instead, gifts us back the power to define our own worth.

Lilith has become a guide for me, a beacon for what is possible when you embrace who you are. My worth is not based upon my capacity or desire to have children; it is based upon my own internal barometer of worth.

Am I living my life in line with my values?

Do I feel fulfilled by my own standards of what that means to me?

Am I aligning my actions with my intentions so that I can feel successful in my own right?

73

As a childfree woman, I know that society is not going to automatically define my worth for me. I have reached the glorious point in my life now where I no longer need to seek out that validation. I create my own value and sense of worth because I know who I am.

I know I am an edge dweller and that is fine. I enjoy that sense of being 'other' because it gives me secrets and mysteries to weave into my story. I walk my own path and it is indeed one full of magic and fulfilment.

I have released the need for someone else to deem me worthy or not – only I can decide that for myself, and I wholeheartedly, and with great joy have decided that I Am Worthy.

Sadie Tichelaar - There is so much possibility for women to achieve and I know you are capable of incredible things. I believe that womanhood does not equal motherhood and I feel it's my mission to enable and inspire childfree women to feel empowered, sovereign, and purposeful. And I think you feel the same way too...

www.thiscuriouslifecoaching.com/

SARAH

At the time of writing this chapter, I am 53 years and 3 months old.

While pondering the theme of being worthy, and how not feeling worthy might have affected me, it occurred to me that for at least 47 of those years I have been living in a state of survival, with a scarcity mindset and a need for approval from others.

I do not remember exactly when that started, or why.

I grew up in a dysfunctional family (normal for the early 1970's). Bullied at home and at school; always the 'good' child. Shy and quiet. Happy in my own space, living in my imagination. I loved reading and writing, poems, and stories; to roller skate, dance, sing and act; to draw, paint, and sew; to be creative. I was happy alone. I felt safe that way.

People brought danger. Anger, aggression, upset, forced opinions, violence. I learned to read micro expressions and body language intuitively. I tried my best to stay out of reach. Sometimes it worked, sometimes it did not. A child in harm's way does not have much to offer in the form of defence. Dissociation became useful, leaving my physical body for a time was easy.

I always knew I was different. I believed the fairy stories. That I must have been stolen by elves from a rich and influential family. Or that I was a Princess, cursed to live outside of the safe and protected land of my birth right (a good analogy of not being in connection with our source energy), or that I was from another planet. Left here by aliens for some reason (this seems more likely to be true as I learn more about Starseeds!).

I never thought being different was 'bad' - not until later.

As a small child I was aware of intuitive nudges that showed me ways to avoid potential dangers. Cross the road here, do not use the underpass, keep away from that person/those people.

As I grew into a teenager, I stopped listening to those nudges and started to pay attention to the people I was forced to spend time with. My family, school mates, friends, teachers, work mates from my after-school job. But everything they were telling me felt wrong.

- Get a job.
- Get a boyfriend.
- Get Married.
- Have Children.
- Live in a semi-detached house

What does all this have to do with being worthy?

Those ideas did not seem right for me. But I did not have the confidence to stand alone. Every time I suggested doing things differently, I was told I was weird, crazy, mad, stupid, not capable, too fat, not pretty enough, that's a man's job, women cannot/do not do that.

But I knew, *just knew,* in my heart I was right. Despite this, I also knew that it was safer to try to fit in. But everything I did to try and fit in felt wrong. *I felt wrong.*

My romantic relationships were a disaster. I lurched from one abusive situation to another, masking any hurt and feelings of abandonment with alcohol. I was definitely a problem drinker.

On a trip to India with a friend, I realised that people are just people. Some good, some not. As cliched as it may sound, I realised, wherever you go - YOU are there.

On my 25th birthday, I woke up in a rented room alone, and burst into tears. I remember thinking, 'I am nearly dead, and I have nothing to show for my life' (yes, I was that dramatic). I cried all day. At this point I *knew* I was not good enough. Nothing I did was good enough. Nobody cared about me.

I had thought about death many times, in a curious way. But on that day I wondered why I was alive at all.

Then, while driving in North Wales, between Capel Curig and Llanberis, on the way to Snowdon, I had an epiphany. Looking at that glorious landscape I realised just how insignificant I was.

Something about that statement seemed to awaken something inside me. Even with depression engulfing me - I felt that knowing that I had felt as a child. I was safer alone. Being alone would save me. Listening to myself would be my salvation. I surrendered and affirmed that I was no longer available for relationships that were not perfect for me. A month later, I met the man who would become my husband!

I wish I could tell you that that was when I realised, I was worthy, and we lived happy ever after - but it is not what happened.

Although I remained haunted by my conviction that I was not good enough, I now had a relationship that was worthy, with a great partner. We shared a desire to explore our spirituality and we trained together in Reiki, Health Kinesiology, NLP and Hypnotherapy.

We have supported each other for 28 years, and we are still happily married despite all that life has thrown at us.

6 years ago, 6 weeks after the death of my father, my husband suffered major health problems and I became his full-time carer. It felt like a double bereavement. Although my husband was alive, he was a very changed person. I found myself in a darker place than the day I woke up questioning my existence on my 25th birthday.

My own health began to suffer, and I was diagnosed with a chronic health condition which meant I was unable to work in the way I was used to. I was deeply unhappy, lost and had no idea how I was going to cope.

Sitting alone in the hospital chapel, with my husband in intensive care, I once again heard that inner voice. 'You are alone, but you are connected. All is well. You can do this; you have all you need inside you.'

I began to meditate again; I journaled every day. I became aware of those intuitive nudges I had as a child. Tentatively I started to follow them.

I stumbled across people on Facebook teaching Law of Attraction and began practicing what they taught. I joined a membership site and began to practice things that were being taught. I began to believe. Not only in the connection of the Universe, of Source energy - but in myself!

In a discussion about my life's purpose, I remember saying, 'I know what I am being called to do, but I do not want to do it,' and I began searching for other things that I could do to be successful and fulfilled in life.

I know what I'm being called to do *but I'm not good enough to do it…*

Through daily practice, I began to accept my calling; to reconnect to my intuitive healing abilities and to hold space for people; to allow deep healing to occur. I knew that I had to revisit all those limiting beliefs and heal the traumas I carried.

For the past year, I have focussed on healing myself. I invested in finding the right people to work with; become part of communities that I would never had thought I could be part of. I have been following my intuition and doing the work I needed to do to become the person I was always meant to be; the slightly weird one who sees things differently; who can look at you and know the truth about your situation; and who can sit with you while you explore those difficult truths.

I am walking my path, taking action, even when I am afraid because I trust my inner guidance. I know that I always have me.

At last, I know, that I AM WORTHY and, my dear Sister, I know that SO ARE YOU.

Sarah Williams is an Intuitive Guidance, Healing & Empowerment Coach for women, individually & in Sacred Circles.

FB @SarahsHealingSpace

SHVETA

'Who do you think you are to write this?'

My inner monologue shrieked at me when I decided to write this chapter. I trembled as a bolt of energy hit every cell in my body with sensations of doubt and disbelief, pressuring me to stop right there and then.

But here I am, untethering my feelings of unworthiness. Marching ahead to write regardless of that voice screaming in my head.

'What is WORTH?' I wondered.

To many, WORTH is an essential commodity. We measure its value based on an imagined measurement of profit, comfort, luxury.

But we are not commodities, so why do we use a similar measuring stick to gauge *our* WORTH?

'When did humans become commodities?' I pondered.

Growing up, I learned that there were many different ways to achieve worthiness:

- My behaviour defines my worth. I need to be perfect.
- My achievements, people's opinions, and accolades are what make me worthy.
- I always have to achieve a high standard to be worthy and feel good about myself.
- If love does not come directly to me, I will do whatever I can to feel needed and appreciated. Appreciation makes me feel worthy.

- When I perform well, I am appreciated by my caretakers. And I feel loved. This helps me feel worthy.
- I always need to showcase my value. Whether in a relationship or a job. That is how I will be able to feel great about myself.
- To feel worthy, I need to gain love by all means in the form of accolades, rewards, appreciation, awards, medallions, trophies, most followers, most likes on social media, most friends, etc.

Deep down, the vibration of worth is feeling loved. The fundamental human essence we are born with - LOVE. But as we start living this human experience, we adopt multi-faceted beliefs based on culture, society, families, etc.

Growing up in a dysfunctional family (something my family would deny, and that's ok) I came to believe that WORTHINESS depended on some external factor; a measuring bar; a standard to be met; a way to behave; a way to show up, etc.

I followed these 'rules' to the letter; be valuable to my employer; be good to my family, and be helpful to my friends. And I associated my worth with that invisible measuring stick, which was then passed to others to use to judge my worthiness.

So, where does this association start?

When love does not come easily to us as children, either due to emotionally unavailable parents or caretakers, wounded or depressed parents, or bedridden caregivers, we find ways to attract love and attention so we can feel great about ourselves. We begin associating our worth with how valuable we are to others, letting everyone around us decide how worthy we are.

I was no different, churning through the ups and downs of life with an urge to be seen, to be heard, to be loved by people around me. My powerful desire for love had me automatically moulding myself to fit in with other people's needs.

I focused on drawing attention and love from others. Weighing the amount of love I received on a scale, to balance with how good I felt about myself.

But no matter how hard I tried, I *never* felt good about myself. This pattern repeated in all my relationships for decades. What stood out in all of them was the instability, the fickleness, and the mercy I sought elsewhere. I suppose I set myself up for failure as I realized that we cannot measure the invisible. Since I associated my worth with accomplishments, accolades and people, there was no stability in that.

I was constantly searching for validation, the approval of others in all spheres of my life- my job, marriage, assets, wealth, physical appearance, financial status, education; the list goes on. I was at the mercy of everything around me so that I could feel good about myself

How did UNWORTHINESS feel?

- I am not good enough to be selected for this job.
- I do not deserve a pay rise.
- I do not deserve a good partner.
- I do not think people like me.
- No one cares about me.
- People give me that look as if they want me to leave.
- I cannot do anything right.
- I need to prove that I am good enough.

And many more

Rest assured, when I was in that mode, I did not see a problem in drawing my worth from others. It was only after healing those wounds of unworthiness, rejection, and not feeling good enough about myself, that I could see how dysfunctional it is to keep handing over our WORTH to others.

So, what do I feel *now* about my WORTH?

- The very essence of me being on this planet is showcasing my worth.
- I was worthy enough. I was chosen to live this life.
- Remember, when we were babies, we did not question our worth. We did not think that 'Ooh! I just soiled my clothes, so I am not good enough to be caressed.' OR 'Ooh! I just farted and burped! So, I am not worthy of being held by my caregivers.'
- My soul chose me this lifetime- isn't that something to celebrate?
- Regardless of the million thoughts screaming at us that we are unworthy, there is an eternal gentle whisper of HIM that tells it all. ONE who gave us this breath and who disagrees with all the negative voices.

- You do not need to do a thing to prove you are good enough, worthy enough, valuable enough, or beneficial enough. Your essence says it all.

Know your worth, loved ones.
I know there is a lot that we may need to change because we are taught the other way. But one step at a time- you will realize that it is time to lose the dysfunctional beliefs that no longer serve you.

So, if I say, YOU ARE WORTHY, because YOU ARE. Would you agree?

Shveta S is an intuitive therapist, an inspired writer, columnist, speaker and creator of Untethered Goddess. Her programs and sessions help women to unleash/connect to their inner goddess, releasing the energetic blocks and trauma leading them to live with authenticity, freedom and exuberance.

www.untetheredgoddess.com

TIERRA

You Are Worthy to Rebuild

Rebuilding may mean different things to different people.

Rebuilding to me means that something happened in your life that caused you to have to pivot; that caused time to stand still when something unexpected occurred. Something that was more than likely unwelcome and caused a life shift. When these types of events occur, we are often unprepared and do not have the mindset it takes to be COURAGEOUS enough to rebuild.

For me, being brave enough to end my second long-term relationship with a narcissist did not necessarily correlate with having the confidence to rebuild a life after. I was confronted by self-doubt, a harsh inner critic and fear about the unknown when attempting to put the pieces back together because we are rarely taught what to do when problems arise in our lives, careers, or relationships.

There is some guidance out there but, it is not nearly what most of us need, or specific to the problems and issues we face. Like a lot of people, I did not even know that narcissistic personality disorder existed, let alone what to do to help myself. Or, how to rebuild my life, finances, and career after I left. I went from being a family to being a single mom on my own that wanted and needed to find a way to financially support myself.

I did not just need to find a way to rebuild my life and earn a living on my own. I also needed to rebuild myself. Rebuilding can impact our self-esteem, self-worth, and identity, making one question their value and worth even if we do not have control over a situation, or intend for it to happen. One of the biggest obstacles was truly believing that I was worthy -- worthy to have what I wanted in life, to be the woman I wanted to be and to create a life I love.

If you asked yourself today, right now, if you truly believe you are worthy to have all that you want in life, would you have any doubts or hesitation? Most people do. And, for those who have endured a high conflict relationship, it can be even more so.

I am here to tell you that you *can* rebuild, and, most of all, that you deserve to. You were created to have a big, beautiful life. You were not put on this earth to settle for less than what you want and need. You were born to thrive. It does not mean it will always be easy, or that you will not have struggles or challenges. But you are worthy. And, with the right tools and action, you can have all that you desire. You can be the woman you want to be, in a life you truly love and want to have. I am living proof of this, and so are my clients. We have all had to rebuild, and we are all rebuilding -- with success, happiness, and confidence. It might not seem possible to you today, but it is possible.

It begins with asking yourself what you truly want. What kind of life would you like to have? What does it look like? Who are the people in it? What experiences do you want to have? How will you feel when you have these things? What will it help you be capable of? I know how hard it can be to imagine and dream. But you can and *should*. Ask yourself these questions and let yourself answer without any limits. Do not be afraid to think big and imagine the biggest possibilities for yourself.

For me, it was to build a seven+ figure career; to provide a life for my boys and me, and to impact women positively. There was a time I could barely bring myself to think this might be possible. Today, it is exactly what I am doing in my life. Finding these answers is the first step to finding yourself, and rebuilding. It is the foundation of your ability to take the next step. When you know these answers, you are already on your way.

Next, you want to identify where you may have limiting beliefs; where you think you are not worthy, capable, or deserving. Instead of letting these beliefs hold you back, or make you doubt what is possible for you, understand that they are just mental programming you received in the past. Our society, media, parents, and other people around us help shape our beliefs.

Doubts and limiting beliefs are normal. Best of all, they can be changed! What we think and believe is always in our power and our control. So, let's find where yours lie and let's start to release those limiting beliefs to replace them with something that serves your highest good.

For example, do you feel you are not capable of earning financial wealth? If so, why? What makes you think you can't? Ask yourself this with every doubt or limiting belief you encounter. Instead of automatically assuming something is not possible, ask yourself, what if it is possible? What if you could have the things you want?

Now, do not get discouraged if it is hard to counter your doubts and limiting beliefs at first. Even the most successful coaches, athletes, CEOs, celebrities, and other accomplished people struggle with doubt and limiting beliefs. The difference is that they work to counter it. They constantly work to change their mind to believe they can have what they want and are capable, and worthy. That is exactly what you can do as well. I did not just come out of my abusive relationships believing I could make my own money or afford to live the life I wanted to live. I had plenty of doubts, fears, and uncertainties! But I worked to shift those limiting beliefs.

Last, find support and resources. Hire a coach, read books, take online courses. The more you empower yourself, the more empowered you will be. That is when we step into our power to create what we need and want in our lives, feeling worthy of it all!

Tierra Womack, MBA, founder of The Brave Way, is a serial, multi-platform mompreneur of 16 years whose businesses have generated over 7-figures. As a Confidence and Wealth coach, Tierra helps female solo entrepreneurs take their businesses to the next level to generate more success with less time, for greater freedom, abundance and prosperity.

www.thebravewaytribe.com

WENDY

The Oxford dictionary defines Worthy as 'Deserving effort, attention, or respect.' How many of us believe that we are deserving of any of these? Well, I for one had many underlying beliefs that I was not worthy of any of them.

I guess my limiting beliefs started when I got to senior school. I had done very well at Junior school. So much so, that I was given a place at a Grammar School. At that time this was seen as a huge achievement. However, when I got there, I was completely out of my depth and felt overwhelmed.

We covered subjects that I had never heard of, Latin, Physics, Chemistry, Biology. I was hopeless at Maths which was at a completely different level to what I had been used to. I did not get it. My dad tried to help me, but to be honest much of it was also beyond him. I did well in non-academic subjects. I loved art, sewing and home economics. I guess that kept me going.

I never got any extra support. I felt the teachers thought I was too stupid to bother with. I was not worthy of their attention. I got through school by making myself invisible. Daydreaming and looking out of the window during lessons. I fell more and more behind, and I just knew I was thick, stupid, and incapable of doing this work. When it came to exams, I would often just put my name at the top of the page and then doodle, wondering why I bothered to turn up.

Life at home was extremely difficult too. Completely chaotic with no support. But somehow I got through school. I could not wait to leave; to move on with my life. When I look back, I laugh. I could not do maths; I was stupid. But somehow, I managed to get myself a reasonable job as an office junior in an accounts department.

Someone believed in me and gave me a fantastic opportunity. I quite enjoyed the role and realised that I was really good with figures. I loved the challenge of balancing spreadsheets. A few years later we got a new accountant, a young guy who was quite forward-thinking. He talked to me about gaining some qualifications and said that the Company would pay for it; I agreed. This kick-started a new love of learning.

My boss believed in me; he recognised my potential. But I still had to learn to believe it myself. Over the years I gained lots of qualifications including an HNC in Business, Diplomas in various subjects and Business Analyst qualifications. I gained distinctions in many subjects. But despite all my qualifications I still felt unworthy. Still having to continuously prove to myself that I was not stupid.

I have had some fantastic jobs during my career. I moved on from accounting and into management, and then a Business Transformation team. I worked hard and achieved some great results, but I still suffered from Imposter syndrome, feeling that at any moment I would be found out. That my bosses would realise that I was too stupid to do the job I was doing.

I overcompensated in so many ways. I worked long hours, often the last one to leave the office at night. I worked for several different organisations, eventually ending up in the corporate world of banking. I hated it, felt unfulfilled and unhappy. I managed a difficult and uncooperative team, and each day became a drag. In my late 50's I walked away from the corporate world and became self-employed. Created a spiritual business called Intuitive Life with Wendy Dixon.

In my late 30's I had started to work on my spiritual self. Initially working towards becoming a spiritual medium. It took me longer than most because I did not believe that I was any good at it. Once again, I was fortunate enough to have someone else who could see my potential. My mentor encouraged me to take the next steps until I started to believe that I could.

I continued on the path of learning with my spiritual work; Spiritual Coaching (I had 25+ years of business coaching, I so wanted to bring the spiritual aspect to it), studying mediumship, reiki, crystal healing, counselling to name but a few; I knew I was still trying to prove myself.

I started to wonder who I was trying to prove myself to, I had enough certificates to decorate a room; how many more did I need? My husband accepts me exactly as I am. We met when I was sweet 16 and still at school. He is fully aware of all the battles I have been through. Despite all of that, he loves me unconditionally.

As I continued on my spiritual journey, I recognised that the only person who needs to accept me is me, and I am worthy of all that I have and desire in my life. It was time to silence my inner critic.

I studied Spiritual Law. The first law being the Law of Pure potentiality, which states that we are pure consciousness, spiritual beings. The law tells us that all things are possible and that we are all able to live a life of pure joy and success if we would allow ourselves to live our true life purpose.

It takes time to discover who we truly are, and often we are so busy trying to control the direction of our life/job/relationship that we forget to live in the NOW, to recognise and live in our own power.

Deepak Chopra states, '*A seed doesn't struggle to become a tree, it simply unfolds with grace*'

It grows with effortless effort; it is successful at living its purpose i.e., growing into a tree.

We all have our own definition of what success means to us. For me, I want to be happy living a spiritual life of peace and joy. I never found that with any of the jobs I had before.

The universe guides us to where we need to be. But if we are not listening, perhaps because we are too busy focussing on the future, we will not see or hear what is right under our nose; the infinite possibilities of what we can achieve. As you awaken spiritually, you begin to recognise those signs and step into your own power.

We can help to support this by spending time in silence, in meditation and in nature. By linking into that higher consciousness, we can access all the wisdom that is held within that universal consciousness. One of the biggest steps in this process is to stop judging. Because judgement of self, or others, destroys the flow of possibility.

I still love to learn. I will never stop learning, but I now accept that I am enough, I am worthy of love and respect, and I shine my light brightly as I live my true spiritual life purpose.

Wendy Dixon is an Author, Spiritual Coach & Psychic medium on a mission to create an online community raising the collective consciousness. Wendy took her own leap of faith moving from one end of the country to another, following guidance from her Spirit team; Leaving behind a secure 9-5 job and moving 100's of miles to create a movement awakening people to their Spiritual gifts and growing their Spiritual awareness. A chance conversation led to Wendy attending a mediumship programme and she knew straight away that she had found her purpose in life. 'I often regret not listening to my intuition, when I do listen to my intuition, I have been amazed to know that this guidance lies within us, always keeping us safe and on the right track and I am so passionate about waking others up to their own intuition and encouraging them to begin to trust the messages coming through. I was guided to move to a different part of the country and to step away from a corporate career, and my life has unfolded in such a beautiful way and I am truly living my purpose in life. The intuitive mind is a sacred gift, and the rational mind is a faithful servant. We have created a society that honours the servant and has forgotten the gift and I am here to remind people.'

www.wendydixon.co.uk

IVY

What do you think of when you hear the word worth? Self-worth? What does that mean to you?

Up until a few months ago I never gave it much thought. It was something I brushed over, non-essential. As if I had all the self-worth in the world but quite the contrary was true. I was underselling, undervaluing, and not giving myself, or the work I do, the value it deserves. I even went as far as to tell my husband that maybe we should not get this amazing new fancy electric car that we had pre-ordered.

So many levels of worth not being recognized in my life.

This car, Ghostrider we call her, is not just any car. It is a Mustang Mach E. Am I a car person? No, not really. But this car stands for something. It represents my beliefs and lifestyle on so many levels. All-electric; light carbon footprint; beautiful design. And yes, I do like nice things. Dare I say I like luxury.

Am I worthy of luxury items such as this? I felt uncomfortable when my husband talked about this car. I was excited, yes, but at the same time, I felt as though I did not deserve it.

I began to process the push-pull I felt about the car. From 'I want it and I deserve it', to 'I don't know if I want something that nice'. As this process continued there was a delay in the delivery of the car. I welcomed the delay with a sigh of relief. I did not have to accept such a fancy item into my life just yet.

Finally, a day after a new client signed up for my program, and my energy was high, I got a call that the car was ready. I had moved into a place where I felt like I deserved this! Everything was totally aligned. Even with that alignment it still took a few weeks until it really felt like mine.

Here is the journal entry I wrote of my breakthrough day when the outer world and my inner world reflected similar things:

'For the 1st time today, I finally felt like I was joyriding in my new car. I had Prince (RIP) blasting on my Bang and Olufsen speakers. I was singing and dancing, showing and feeling my joy at every traffic light. I got to park in the Electric Cars Only spots at the mall, upfront and easy. I was told I was a cool mom by the young guy working at the covid testing site where my daughter had to get tested for school.

It almost felt as if I could be joyriding with a girlfriend or two, whipping around town having an adventure. Alas, there were no friends. It was me, in the front seat and my two mini-me sidekicks in the back. There was this elevated level of excitement, fun and power as I drove like I knew what I was doing. I wanted to go fast and was proud of my ride. I felt like I owned my suburban town.

It wasn't until halfway through my drive that I had to remind myself, "I own a Mustang and I am ******* Worthy!"

A MUSTANG!!!!

A Mustang Mach E for the win! Its electric baby! I say 'goodbye' to Dinosaur Gas Stations and 'Hello!' to my new everyday luxury of saving the Earth in Style. This is aligned with who I am and what I stand for!'

Have you ever felt like you were not ready, or worthy enough, to own an expensive material item? Or to treat yourself to a service or something nice? Maybe you have been undercharging, not fully recognizing your value.

If any of this applies to you know that it does not have to be this way. It can change. Start with your mindset. Observe without judgement and see how you can shift your perspective.

As I level up my life and step into my power and purpose, I step on fear and know that I deserve this.

I can maintain this car by generating money I earn in my business.

I declare I make money doing what I love, helping people cultivate a balanced life through a daily yoga practice and expressing themselves freely through their unique talents.

When I told my husband how I drove around town that day he asked me if I felt like a pilot's wife driving around in the car. I told him yes, but in my heart and saying now the answer is no. I felt like a yoga teacher & coach stepping into the limelight of her career. I realize now that is His worth and mine is the latter.

Know your worth!

I am worthy and I love and deserve my Electric Mustang!

Ivy Glass is an Integration Coach, fusing yoga + coaching for powerful results for the mind, body & spirit. She teaches her signature Kundalini Vinyasa Flow classes online and in person, hosts wellness events & retreats. She teaches all types of people from children, pregnant mamas, families & women's groups. Her all-inclusive Pajama Disco Yoga Party is a fun approach to yoga anyone can connect too! Ivy's goal is to teach people how to Stop, Drop & Yoga!

https://linktr.ee/IVyoga

ALLSAMA

Has someone ever told you, 'You are worthy'?

Sitting on a stool at the kitchen counter for dinner, my 6-year-old son was staring at his food lost in thought. When asked, he said, 'I wish I did not exist'. Hearing these words from my son at such a tender age broke my heart.

He revealed that while playing at school the week before, he had had a disagreement with a good friend. He was told that he was not good enough and very bad, and something more.

Having experienced this kind of situation in the past, I was able to explain to him that he cannot be good OR bad at the same time. We are all good AND bad. Someone telling me I am bad does not mean that I am ALL bad.

Have you ever thought about what makes us feel unworthy? It is the fear of being COMPARED. This fear is embedded in everything we do from the day we are born. In every aspect of our daily lives, every task that we do.

A child grows up hearing constantly that he or she is not good enough for something. If he is not given constructive feedback, he grows up with a sense of needing to prove something. Not to himself, but to others.

A teenager wants to prove his worth to be in an elite group of friends he is fascinated with.

An employee feels embarrassed to reveal what he feels to be a lower rank employment status to a friend that he believes holds a better, more important position.

A father is continuously working and stressing about raising the status of his family in comparison to others.

A husband, with an ever demanding and unsatisfied family, feels that he is not good enough for them.

A wife is so submerged in the judgements that her family has created for her, she is no longer able to see that she really is enough!

A lover constantly fears being unworthy in eyes of his beloved and forgets the power of accepting the way they are.

And so, the list goes on...

Has someone ever told you that 'You are worthy'?

Do you feel relieved and happy when you hear that? Do you rely on a statement like this, or assurance from others to make you feel better?

Do you really not know yourself, your beautiful inner self?

My journey from childhood saw me go from being a very introverted, shy child to being a somewhat extroverted adult. Like everyone there were many experiences, rejections, acceptance, self-doubt, self-motivation, feeling inferior and sometimes superior. Until finally feeling spiritually uplifted and learning not to be affected by what other people think.

As a child, I tried my best to be good to everyone around me, especially my school friends. I remember I used to feel depressed and worried if they were annoyed with me. I carried this habit with me for a very long time. The number of people able to affect my mental peace may have decreased, but I still relied on a few people to help me find happiness and peace. I was looking to them to provide my worthiness.

We, in our unawareness, submit all our worthiness in the eyes of others, forgetting to open the door of our self-realization.

When we receive negativity from others in form of their actions or words, we grab those comments and allow them to hurt us immediately. We forget to think further and deeper. We forget to re-question ourselves.

We cannot make others happy by being bad to them - that is true. We cannot make others happy even when we do no harm to them, and they are still not happy with us. That is also true. The only thing we can do is to remind ourselves that we are beautiful souls and that it is okay if a few people are not happy with us (provided you did no intentional harm). It is their journey, their own learning path.

When we emotionally hurt ourselves at that moment, we lose the opportunity to reflect the divine invisible light that we can shine on them; we lose the opportunity to send them vibrations of compassion and kindness. Trust me, when something happens that brings you feelings of unworthiness, just relax. The sweetness of that inner peace is worth it!!

My mother always taught me that even if a person is bad to you, there is always something good in them, and we all should try to see that goodness and forget the bad. It reminds me of the theory of being bad and good at the same time. Moreover, there is nothing bad or good in this universe, it is all grey.

There is so much controversy, between ages, between generations, between regions, between cultures and between religions. We all struggle to create good and bad lists.

I AM ENOUGH... is a profound statement. Remember this whenever in doubt!

Birthdays have been very important to me since childhood. It was one special day when I could be happy because everybody would be nice to me. I considered my birthday to be ruined and felt extremely sad if I felt hurt by someone. I was extra sensitive to being treated well or not on that special day. That expectation has decreased as I got older, but it stayed with me for a long time.

Gradually I realized that it was always ME creating rules for my happiness. Always ME preventing me from being calm despite what was going on around me. It always has been ME! I have the right to be happy on my birthday, so I threw out the old me and decided to change my attitude to something more beautiful, more angelic. To remember I AM Worthy! I Am Enough!

You are worthy and a beautiful soul!

You are worthy even when you are wrong and make errors, just be ready to correct them!

You are worthy physically, mentally, and emotionally! All of You!

Allsama B K - is an established Indian classical dance coach cum concept choreographer, and an equally passionate food science tech and food safety professional. Still going on in her long journey of awakening to one's higher self, she wants to spread this light under the open wings of divinity. She finds her peace in uplifting others, is gradually changing her way she used to handle things in the past and a staunch believer of whatever happens, happens for good!! She has a unique combination of art and technology talent. She is fascinated researching about outer space, is happy when she paints or writes. Dance is her meditation, and she loves knowing science with dedication. Her bucket list is full, and this life seems so less for her to learn so many things. A life is worth a shot!

www.facebook.com/acharya.shama.1

55 JOURNAL PROMPTS

Below are 55 journal prompts that will be the beginning of your own journey of reclaiming your worth.

1. Who am I at my core?
2. What is the story of my worth?
3. Who am I before the fear?
4. What would I need to believe about myself in order to reclaim my self-worth?
5. What do I believe is possible for me?
6. What do I desire from life?
7. What stories tell me that these desires are not possible?
8. Who am I committed to being?
9. What lights me up?
10. How can I do more things each day that light me up?
11. What do I love and accept about myself?
12. What would I choose in life if anything were possible?
13. How do I judge myself?
14. What judgment of myself can I let go of today?
15. How do I perceive myself?
16. How would I like to be perceived?
17. What values are important to me and why?
18. Who do I want to become?
19. What needs to shift in the identity of who I think I am now and who I would like to become?
20. If my self-worth is created by the thinking that I focus on, what new thought choices could I make?
21. What are my passions?
22. What does 1 year from now me look like if I continue to believe I am not worthy of certain things in life?
23. If you were a book, what would the reviews say?
24. Where are you handing over your power, saying things like 'If I get this job, get this relationship, get this 'thing' it will mean I am worthy?
25. How can you reclaim that power today?
26. When you tune into your soul and the intuitive part of your being,

what do you hear about your self-worth?

27. If you were born worthy and you have nothing to do to become or be worthy, what changes in your life?

28. What do you tell yourself has to happen or be in place before you can arrive at a sense of feeling 'worthy'?

29. Who are you before any fear?

30. If my beliefs around self-worth act as a lens from which I get to view and experience of myself, what beliefs do I choose to become the new filter?

31. If my beliefs about self-worth were created based upon past moments in time, that are no longer applicable now, what beliefs can I now let go of?

32. What is niggling inside of me, what would I love to do, be, have in life?

33. What matters to you most in life?

34. Where in your life do you feel confident and in flow?

35. How would I know that my life had shaped into how I would love it to be, what would have to have changed or shifted?

36. What am I most grateful for in life?

37. What assumptions do I make about who I am and what I am capable of?

38. How do my actions mismatch my desires in life?

39. If I fully accepted life, myself, everything about me right now, what would that look like?

40. If I felt 100% sure that my thoughts were creating the experience of myself, what beliefs would I let go of that no longer serve me?

41. What does the future version of me that embraces their self-worth and lives a vibrant and confident life have to tell the current version of me?

42. How do you compare yourself to others?

43. What are five amazing things about you?

44. How can you embrace yourself more?

45. If there were no limits in life, anything was possible, what would you do, be, have?

46. What would you most like to accomplish in life?

47. What will be your legacy?

48. What steps can you take today to reclaim your self-worth?

49. What have you triumphed in life?
50. What lessons have your learned from your triumphs?
51. What can you do each day to embody your self-worth?
52. What can become your daily self-worth mantra?
53. How do I demonstrate self-love?
54. What can become my daily self-love mantra?
55. I am a powerful creator, responsible for 100% of my own life and experiences this lifetime – knowing this now, what do I choose to have, be, and do?

ABOUT THE EVERYDAY GODDESS REVOLUTION

Founded by Spiritual Coach, Leanne MacDonald, The Everyday Goddess Revolution are blazing a trail in the world of female empowerment.

Passionate about creating a platform for women to speak their truth, heal their trauma, reclaim their life, and consciously create balance, joy, and adventure in their lives.

We bring women around the world:

Community
Soul-powerment Events
Resources & Programs

Join our Facebook group: www.facebook.com/groups/tedgr

Write in one of our future multi author book projects -
www.theeverydaygoddessrevolution.com/projects

REVIEWS FOR KNOW YOUR WORTH GODDESS

"Sadie's chapter reminds us that we have the power to define our own worth, regardless of the societal narratives we are given. As a childless woman, I felt Sadie's call to embrace the freedom that comes with being an "edge dweller", finding magic and mystery in the wild and less trodden path I'm currently on."

Katy Seppi, Founder, Chasing Creation

"Reading these words on the page, I felt as though Rachel was right there, holding my hand and guiding me through my learning and self-discovery of worthiness. Open, honest, strong and ever-courageous, Rachel lights the path leading to deeper connection with yourself and your own present and future wellbeing. The power of Rachel's words hammer home the possibilities you always dreamt of yet didn't dare believe…. well, now's the time to believe!"

Hannah Bunce

"Allsama's story demonstrates the power of finding self-worth in everyday dialogues with ourselves and with people we love. A heart-touching and though-provoking essay"

- Shilpa Mudiganti

"Loretta's triumphant journey from adversity to worthiness and self-love is an inspiration to us all! Her courage and determination shine a guiding light to find our own healing path."

-Robin Williams, Chakra Gemstone Jewelry Designer

"Miriam Husby Stener writes poetical about worthiness in the book,

This chapter gave me a little time of breathe and reminded me that no matter how I feel, my worthiness is real. Let Miriam's words remind you that you got nothing to prove, you Are 100% worthy your body and soul."

- Eli Romstad Helgemo

"This is a very powerful read. I highly recommend this book for anyone who has ever had to fight to rediscover themselves and rebuild their life from a traumatic experience. Tierra's chapter really helped me to know I am worthy and the hard work to start over is worth it. I feel very settled and at peace after reading this book. A great gift for anyone who you know is struggling right now!!"

-Renee Robinson

"A relatable, honest and raw share. So much of our worthiness is tied up in the workings of our parental relationships and Emma brings hers to the table beautifully. It got me thinking about mine in a whole new way!"

- Kathy Bell, Breathwork Facilitator and Soul Connection Guide

I am honoured to write a review for this marvellous soul warming chapter by Shveta SC. There are so many pearls of wisdom in what she has written, for me personally it stirs soul memories pertaining to self-worth. This inspiring Author has touched on the very essence of what it takes to be worthy, we need to undo the negativity that society has instilled in us and caused our heart, minds and souls to forget, Shveta has tapped into the very essence of worthiness and reminds us that we are glorious and WORTHY just as we are...truly beautiful words from a gifted writer who speaks from her heart and soul.

-Jasmin Baljak(Success and Performance Coach to World Leaders)

"Wendy's story is a fascinating touching real life tale of hope and self realisation. . Its accessibility to relate to every person who experiences such trauma and self doubt is so honest and true that it gives hope to people who feel worthless and lost. It is a real Inspirational journey that enables a glimpse of positive possibilities that everyone can achieve if they dare to look beyond what us holding them back and the blocks that bar their way in taking a leap of faith into their true self. Just beautiful."

 - Karen

"Nicola provides a wonderful and thought-provoking insight into the meaning of worthiness and unconditional love. She enriches the discussion with great effect by sharing her own life experiences which helps the reader relate to the subject. The addition of the story in the dark forest leaves a lasting impression."

-Susan Knight

I was captivated by Karishma's powerful personal story which explores her journey from feeling undervalued and 'not good enough', to totally claiming her worthiness and value! Inspirational and totally relatable, I am sure we can all learn from Karishma's experience, and how, with self-acceptance and self-connection, she demonstrates for others what is possible!

-Fiona Drake, Mindset Coach and Speaker

"Only we can name our worth. We teach others our value. Our worth is defined by how we view ourselves. Your worth is 100% from within. This is an incredibly powerful, 'stop you in your tracks' knowing from wise woman Hillary Sepulveda. Take note and just do it!!"

-Sunne Justice, author of "Mugged By God"

"After reading her remarkable journey from being bullied as a child, to the strong, brave and powerful woman she is today, Sarah is an inspiration to us all. This is very thought provoking too regarding the unbelievable "shoulds" that society throws our way."

-Camille Plews, Business Mentor

"Buckso has a great understanding of the mind and how this impacts on our lives and self-esteem. With her open honesty she takes us on a journey into discovering her true self, through her internal struggles that she has endured and worked on, that make her the confident, powerful woman that she is today."

-Jean Eatoe, Holistic Therapist

"Like all the best teachers Haley's message is simple and powerful; you are sacred. And the world is blessed to have you in it, taking up space.

Haley, like so many of us, knows that walking away from unworthiness is incredibly hard, an ever-changing challenge. To love yourself fully is no easy path, but she reminds us with her beautiful writing (and teaching) that it will be the most important one you'll ever walk…."

Sarah Robinson, Yoga Teacher and Author of 'Yoga for Witches' and 'Yin Magic'

Printed in Great Britain
by Amazon

64200477R10068